HOW CAN A

GOOD GOD

LET BAD THINGS

HAPPEN?

HOW CAN A GOOD GOD LET BAD THINGS HAPPEN?

MARK TABB

NAVPRESS

NAVPRESS ⦿

NavPress is the publishing ministry of The Navigators, an international Christian organization and leader in personal spiritual development. NavPress is committed to helping people grow spiritually and enjoy lives of meaning and hope through personal and group resources that are biblically rooted, culturally relevant, and highly practical.

For a free catalog go to www.NavPress.com
or call 1.800.366.7788 in the United States or 1.800.839.4769 in Canada.

ISBN-13: 978-1-60006-268-1
ISBN-10: 1-60006-268-7

Cover design by The DesignWorks Group, Jeff Miller, www.thedesignworksgroup.com

Some of the anecdotal illustrations in this book are true to life and are included with the permission of the persons involved. All other illustrations are composites of real situations, and any resemblance to people living or dead is coincidental.

Unless otherwise identified, all Scripture quotations in this publication are taken from the *Holy Bible*, New Living Translation, ©1996. Used by permission of Tyndale House Publishers Inc., Wheaton, Illinois 60189. All rights reserved. Other versions used include: the HOLY BIBLE: NEW INTERNATIONAL VERSION* (NIV*). Copyright © 1973, 1978, 1984 by International Bible Society. Used by permission of Zondervan Publishing House. All rights reserved; *THE MESSAGE* (MSG). Copyright © 1993, 1994, 1995, 1996, 2000, 2001, 2002, 2005. Used by permission of NavPress Publishing Group.

Library of Congress Cataloging-in-Publication Data

Tabb, Mark A.
  How can a good God let bad things happen? / Mark Tabb.
      p. cm.
  Includes bibliographical references.
  ISBN-13: 978-1-60006-268-1
  ISBN-10: 1-60006-268-7
  1. Bible. O.T. Job--Criticism, interpretation, etc. 2. Suffering--Biblical teaching. I. Title.
  BS1415.52.T33 2008
  231'.8--dc22

                              2008022958

Printed in the United States of America

1 2 3 4 5 6 7 8 / 12 11 10 09 08

For Valerie

CONTENTS

ACKNOWLEDGMENTS

Many, many people play a part in moving a book from an idea swirling around in a writer's head to the printed page. First and foremost, I would like to thank Gary Terashita who pushed and prodded me to make this book far better than I ever could have on my own. I cannot put into words how much I value your friendship and the impact you have had on my life and career.

I would also like to thank Liz Heany, who took what I thought was a pretty good book and found ways to make it even better. Liz, you are absolutely the best at what you do. Thank you for once again making me a better writer.

To Kris Wallen, Caleb Seeling, and the rest of the NavPress family, thank you for once again allowing me to partner with you. I thank God for you.

To Pastor Mark Wright and Brandywine Community Church, I cannot express the depths of gratitude I have for you, especially when it comes to this book. Your words of encouragement, and the stories of how God used the original incarnation of this book in your lives, have both sustained and humbled me. Over the past few years this book has become as much yours as it is mine. Thank you.

Above all, all praise to the God of all comfort "who comforts us in all our troubles so that we can comfort others. When others are troubled, we will be able to give them the same comfort God has given us. You can be sure that the more we suffer for Christ, the more God will shower us with his comfort through Christ" (2 Corinthians 1:4-5).

INTRODUCTION

I t has been said that every great book begins with a question. I am not claiming greatness for this book, but it, too, began with a question. Actually, it began with a series of questions spread out over many years. And those questions always came back to one central theme: suffering. However, the question I found myself asking regarding suffering through the years was not the great philosophical dilemma with which great men and women have wrestled for millennia. I don't know why, but I have never asked why there is suffering in the world or why God would allow suffering. Perhaps some long-forgotten childhood experience left my mind too warped to ask such an obvious question. No, the question I found myself coming back to time and again was always less philosophical and more rhetorical. The question that launched me on the journey that resulted in this book was simply: Why not suffering? Or, more to the point, why should I or anyone else be exempt from the suffering that has enveloped the human race since the first man and woman rejected God in favor of sin?

I know, I know. Let the howls of protest begin. I sound as though I am minimizing the pain and horror that has marked the history of the human race since the dawn of time. Believe me, that is not my intention. I am writing this preface nearly five years after I first wrote the book you are about to read. Since its original release, many people have come to me and shared their own stories of suffering. At times, I can hardly stand to listen, not because my heart is hard but because it breaks for those on whom life has thrown such a horrific burden. As if that were not enough, God has recently focused my attention upon stories from the Holocaust. After reading Elie Wiesel's classic work *Night*, I almost contacted my publishing company to cancel this book. Wiesel's true story haunts me, and it will haunt me until the day I die, as well it should. Reading how he and his family suffered unspeakable cruelties at the hands of other human beings, I realized how little I or anyone I know understands about suffering. Yet human history has shown that the atrocities of the Holocaust are not unique, neither in the past nor in the future. That thought chills me to the bone. How could I or any thinking human being minimize the horror of suffering?

Nor am I saying that suffering is part of the human experience, so deal with it. Such a fatalistic approach is an unnatural thought in the minds of creatures created in the image of God. Perhaps this is why suffering creates such a dilemma for members of the human race. Since time began — or, more accurately, since sin entered the world — death and suffering have been part and parcel of the human experience. Romans 5:12 tells how Adam's sin brought death to the entire human race. Not only does this explain why everyone dies, it also tells us why the stench and power of death is wrapped around the entire world. Yet even though everyone dies and even though suffering has defined human existence since the day Adam and Eve brought death down on all their descendants, death and pain and agony always feel like invaders when they strike us or someone we love. We recoil against them and scream out in anger. Our reaction shows that all of us know we weren't made for this. We were not made for a world filled with heartache and sorrow, yet we've never known any other world. That is why we wonder how a good God could allow bad things to happen. When bad things strike, our hearts long for a world free of such needless and mindless suffering. And the questions begin pouring from our hearts toward heaven. *How, God?* we ask. *How could you let this happen?*

And that's the question I plan to explore in the pages that follow. I want to explore the question of how, not why. How could God let bad things happen? is not a question of indictment against God but a question of wonder. What I really want to know is this: How did we get in this place where suffering is such a natural and normal part of life yet feels so unnatural and abnormal? But that's only a small part of the equation. The bigger question that lies behind it is this: Can I continue to trust a God who claims to be good if he will not exempt me from the pain and suffering of this cruel world? And if I can muster up a yes to that question, I still face a litany of others. I will not list them all here. They await you on the pages that follow. They are not questions I made up. Rather, they are questions I've heard in hospital waiting rooms and at accident scenes and in intensive care wards over the past twenty-plus years during my work first as a pastor and now as a fire department chaplain.

Yet this book is not merely a book of questions. It is, above all, a book written not for those who want to consider the question of suffering on a philosophical level but for those who face it on a daily basis. I wrote this book for my friends who lost their seventeen-year-old daughter more than a decade ago and to this day continue to feel the void her death left behind. I wrote this book for the wife and mother whose husband abandoned her because he did not want to be pinned down by the responsibilities of being a husband and father. I wrote this book for the friend whose wife suddenly died after more than thirty years of marriage, leaving him lost and disoriented without her. And I wrote this book for the little boy who cries in the dark as his parents fight violently in the other room, thinking he is asleep. Simply put, I wrote this for the person who hurts, as one pilgrim to another, as we try to figure out how to trust the God we know is good as we make our way through a world that is anything but.

There is another question that finally pushed me over the edge and made me start writing this book. It came directly from the pages of the Bible, from the lips of the man who will forever stand as the poster child of suffering. His name was Job and his story can be found in the Old Testament book that bears his name. I will not give away too much of his story here, for I want you to read the rest of this book. However, he asked a question I have not been able to push out of my mind since the day God brought it to my attention through one of my former Bible professors, a godly man named Ken Matthews. Job asked his wife this simple yet profound question. On the day the two of them lost everything, he turned to her and asked, "Should we accept only good things from the hand of God and never anything bad?" (Job 2:10). You will hear this question reverberate through every page of this book. The question so gripped me that I knew I must use Job and his story as my guide if I were to ever write anything worth reading on a subject as weighty as this. I pray that you will find this book worth reading and that God will use it to grant you grace and healing through the pain you endure—the pain that prompted you to pick up this book and consider how a good God could allow bad things to happen to you.

CHAPTER 1

WE CANNOT CONTROL GOD'S HAND

"As powerful as we are, we have no control over God's hand." That's all the sheriff could say to explain why Stan and Beth and two of their three children died in a freak accident. Given the circumstances, what else could he say? The odds against a ten-ton, one-hundred-year-old tree suddenly uprooting itself at the precise moment a family of five drives by in their Lincoln are astronomical. And for the tree to strike neither the hood nor the trunk but to land squarely on top of the passenger compartment crushing four of the five people inside defies imagination, especially when the car was traveling forty miles an hour.

As I sit in the quiet of my study, typing out these words two weeks later, my mind still struggles to believe that Stan is gone. I keep expecting a chime to sound on my computer, and I'll click the envelope on the corner of the screen to find some lame joke from him in my e-mail inbox. Half the time I found these quips and quotes a little annoying. I don't like forwards. At least, I didn't.

I guess when I go out next week with the surviving members of our group of friends who eat lunch together on a regular basis in order to encourage each other, it will sink in that Stan is gone, because he won't be there. He was always the steady member of the group. The highs and lows of life didn't knock him off balance. Perhaps raising an autistic son kept things in perspective for him. He and Beth worried about the day they would not be there for their son. But that day will never come. They died together because they could not control God's hand.

The question of why they died reverberated through the funeral home last week. Why would God take the life of a pastor and his wife and their ten-year-old son and six-year-old daughter? And why would he leave a four-year-old girl to grow up with nothing but fading memories of her family? I am thankful no one offered any answers. Four caskets lined up across the front of a room made any answer seem insignificant and thoughtless.

The pastor in charge of the funeral compared the deaths of Stan and his family to the tragedy the Old Testament character Job endured. In one day, Job lost everything. Raiding bands of thieves rode in from the desert, carried away all his oxen and donkeys and camels, and killed his servants. Later that day, fire fell from heaven and burned up his flocks and his shepherds. At the same time, a windstorm knocked down his oldest son's house, killing everyone inside, including Job's seven sons and three daughters. As the pastor recounted the story, he added, "Sometimes bad things happen to good people and we never know why. God doesn't offer any explanations. All we can do is continue to trust in God and his goodness and grace."

I looked across the room at the only surviving member of the family and thought, *But Job wasn't four and a half. Job wasn't four and a half.*

Emily is. Emily cried in the dark, pinned in the backseat of the car, unable to move because of the tree. Sounds of rescue workers scrambling to do something surrounded her while one firefighter held her hand and reassured her that everything would be okay. Two days later she was released from the hospital. She keeps asking where her mother and father are. "With Jesus in heaven," she is told. She doesn't understand why she can't be with them, nor does she understand why she cannot go back to the only home she ever knew. Emily's world will never be the same because she has no control over God's hand.

At this point many of us feel compelled to defend God's honor. God didn't cause the tree to fall on Stan and Beth any more than he caused calamity to fall upon Job, we say in God's defense. If anyone is responsible, it has to be Satan. One of my friends told me the Devil had to be pushing hard on that tree to make it fall as Stan and Beth drove by. I guess that makes sense. Stan was doing good work in his church on the east side of Indianapolis, and Satan wanted it stopped.

But Stan's church was small. Why would Satan target him? Will trees soon drop on everyone who tries to make a real difference in the world for Jesus' sake? A renowned pastor in Dallas passed away at the age of ninety-two a few days after Stan died. He never had to dodge any trees. Why didn't Satan take his life years ago if he is indeed in the business of snuffing out the lives of anyone who poses a threat to his kingdom of darkness?

Even if Satan is to blame for Stan's death, something still troubles me. According to the first two chapters of the book of Job, Satan asked for and received God's permission before he could unleash his nightmare on Job. I can't help but ask, is the one who gives permission as culpable as the one who carries out the deed? Insurance companies seem to think they are. They classify such events as trees dropping on cars as "acts of God." So did Job. "The LORD gave me everything I had, and the LORD has taken it away," he cried out as he fell to the ground after hearing that his ten children died together in a tragic accident. "Praise the name of the LORD" (Job 1:21).

I know I'm treading on dangerous ground here. I've already had people object to what you just read and tell me that God didn't cause these tragedies. I agree. He didn't. But in his providence, God did allow them to occur to accomplish his greater purposes. I grew up hearing a lot about the difference between God's permissive will and his causal will. This distinction makes tragedy more palatable while keeping our image of a good God intact. A holy God will not, and cannot, do something evil.

But what if accidental deaths are not evil in the eyes of God? What if total financial ruin is not tragic in his estimation? What if all of the calamities we dread — the nightmare scenarios and worst-case outcomes that keep us up at night worrying — are not worst case but best case to God? If somehow, and God forbid it to be true, that which I fear is the very thing God not only allows but causes, do I really want to follow a God like this?

I can, I am told, because God has a purpose in all trials. Those who find themselves immersed in trials and suffering hear this a lot. The Lord has a reason for everything that happens to those who love him and call upon his name, we're told. To paraphrase Albert Einstein, God isn't playing dice with the universe or with his children. All things work together for his ultimate plan. Good will result from evil. It did for Joseph.

I love the story of Joseph, especially as images of that crushed Lincoln flash in my mind. Joseph was his father's favorite son. Although he was the second-youngest of twelve brothers, he was the first son born to his father Jacob by Jacob's one true love, Rachel. She later died giving birth to Joseph's brother Benjamin. Grief made Jacob even more protective of his favorite son, but no one could protect Joseph from his brothers' jealousy. One day when they were all far from home taking care of the family herds, the ten older brothers seized Joseph, threw him into a hole, and sold him as a slave to the first caravan that happened by. His misfortune did not stop there. As if being a slave wasn't bad enough, Joseph was unjustly accused of rape and thrown into an Egyptian prison to rot away, forgotten.

But God didn't leave him there. A few years after Joseph landed in prison, God caused a chain of events that resulted in Joseph winning his freedom, and then the king of Egypt made him his number-two man. When a drought brought the ten brothers back before Joseph, he told them not to worry for their lives, even though he had the authority to pay them back for what they'd done to him. Instead he told them, "Don't be afraid of me. As far as I am concerned, God turned into good what you meant for evil" (Genesis 50:19-20).

"God turned into good what you meant for evil." Surely the same principle applies to the tragedies the rest of us endure. No matter how evil circumstances may appear on the outside, God can and will turn them into something good. Romans 8:28 turns the principle into a promise: "And we know that God causes everything to work together for the good of those who love God and are called according to his purpose for them." If not for this promise, we could do nothing more than shiver under the covers, afraid of whatever calamity will strike next.

I think I'll keep repeating Romans 8:28 over and over in my head until I feel better, until I can drive down a deserted country road and not wonder if a tree will strike my car, killing four of my five family members. But the more I repeat the verse, the more I am struck by what it does not say. It does not say God has some hidden purpose behind every event that happens in my life, at least not a purpose I will ever see or understand. Nor does the verse tell me I can force something good out of this. I cannot control God's hand, and when I try to force some good purpose onto tragic events, that's exactly what I'm trying to do. God may work for the good of those who have been called according to his purpose, but that doesn't mean you or I will fully understand what that good may be.

And that's the dilemma I really do not want to face. I can accept tragedy when I see God working through it, but will I when I cannot? Job posed this question to his wife: "Should we accept only good things from the hand of God and never anything bad?" He didn't ask how a good God could do such a horrible thing to him. Instead he accepted both his earlier good fortune and the tragic turn his life eventually took as expressions of God's will for his life. I don't know if I can. As I sit here pecking at my keyboard, I wonder if I will ever be able to bring myself to accept bad things from the hand of God without demanding an explanation. Will I stick with him in the midst of a nightmare if I never see any tangible results or ever know why he would allow such pain to be inflicted upon me? Looking at suffering and pain through Job's eyes makes me realize that the question is not whether I will try to understand tragedy or rejoice in it in the hope that spiritual maturity runs through the valley of the shadow. The real question is one I would rather not ask: Will I accept bad things from the hand of God as readily as I accept the good?

Can I take the question a step further? I daily ask for God's guidance. I want his favor and his mercy and his grace and his presence. I'm not alone. All of us want God to bless us and cause his face to shine on us. But at what price? In my years of trying to follow Christ by faith, I've discovered that I feel closest to Jesus when life is the hardest. Am I willing to ask him for hard times because in those times I must exercise real faith? I want his presence, but am I willing to ask for feelings of distance from God in order that I might walk by faith and not emotion? Am I willing to pray, *God, allow tragedy into my life, allow me to suffer, in order that I might understand what your Son went through on the cross*?

Maybe I'm getting ahead of myself. I'll save those questions for the last chapter of this book. For now it is enough to ask, will I continue to believe in him and follow his Son even if doing so never results in any blessings in this life? Will I believe when believing only makes life harder not easier? Will I accept bad things from the hand of God and keep trusting in him even if the bad so overwhelms the good as to make it invisible?

Do I want to explore such questions? Are you kidding? Believe me, this is one aspect of the Christian life I would rather leave untouched. All of us would. Unfortunately, we can't ignore it because it doesn't ignore us. We don't seek tragedy and heartache and tears and asking God why. They seek us. It is not a question of *if* our lives will be turned over by grief but *when*. And when tragedy strikes, when everything around us screams, "God has forgotten you," what will you do?

"Shall we accept only good things from the hand of God and never anything bad?" Job asked his wife. We cannot control God, but will we follow him when his hand strikes rather than caresses?

PART ONE

HOW COULD GOD LET THIS HAPPEN?

Security is the mortal's greatest enemy.

— C. S. LEWIS

CHAPTER 2

PARADISE AND THE PARADOX OF SUFFERING

God put the first man and woman in paradise. He gave them the perfect life—nothing to worry about, everything they ever needed surrounding them. They didn't have to be concerned about coming down with a cold when the weather turned bad because the weather never turned bad and colds did not exist. Neither did the flu or allergies or chicken pox or measles or arthritis or cancer or any other sickness. Their eyesight wouldn't fail when they hit middle age, nor would their gall bladders develop stones. Death did not yet exist. The place teemed with life.

And what a life it was. The man and the woman lived in a perfect relationship with one another and had a perfect relationship with God. They didn't struggle with the distance between heaven and earth, for there was no distance. I'm not sure how everything worked, but God physically walked with Adam and Eve. They lived in the very presence of God without fear. They didn't have to struggle to figure him out from what they read in a book. They saw him, face-to-face. God lived in the center of their existence. Neither God nor the first man and woman had ever known any other way of life on Planet Earth.

Their physical lives weren't so bad either. They enjoyed food without end, a garden paradise for a home, and as for clothes, they didn't need them. Shame didn't make them want to cover up, and God kept the outside temperature at a perfect level. The first man and woman lived in a tropical paradise without the bugs or the sunburn or the crowds. The best the planet could offer lay at their fingertips. The wonders and glories of nature, unstained by human hand, surrounded them. Perfect sunrises. Perfect sunsets. Night skies exploding with stars. Crystal clear streams and rivers. Trees filled to overflowing with the songs of birds. All creation sang praises to God, and the man and woman joined right in.

Paradise. They lived in paradise.

Apparently, it wasn't enough. If it were, they would have stayed. But it wasn't, and they left. Or should I say they were driven out. Evicted. Evicted from paradise because they weren't satisfied with a perfect environment. Somehow they found it difficult to be content with unfettered happiness, even with walking with God. When the serpent told them they could trade places with the Almighty, they fell for his lie. In this perfect world there were only two rules — one spoken, the other unspoken. We all know the only spoken law: Don't eat the fruit from the Tree of Knowledge of Good and Evil. Yet underneath this spoken rule, we can hear God telling the first man and woman the same thing he keeps telling us: "Trust me." He never explained to Adam and Eve why they should stay away from the tree in the middle of the garden. Why should he? That God said it should have been enough. Even when they could see God face-to-face, they had to exercise faith. They chose not to. Sin always begins with unbelief.

If we're going to come to grips with suffering, this is the place to start because this is where suffering came into existence. It all began here. When God created the universe, he stepped back and declared it very good. And it was. Most of it still is. Every time I see another set of photographs sent to Earth by the Hubble telescope, I am awed by the wonder of God's artistry. Scientists will point the Hubble toward some remote corner of the galaxy and find a giant cluster of stars and gases erupting in a dazzling array of color. No artist could paint anything that can compare. Yet there they sit, in a remote corner of space, where no one can enjoy their wonder except God, who hung them there. And I wonder, how can a universe be so beautiful, so spectacular, and, at the same time, so cruel?

The answer goes back to the garden. The first act of sin didn't affect only the first man and woman. All of nature was subjected to God's curse the moment Adam and Eve ate the forbidden fruit (see Romans 8:20). If clocks and calendars had been invented, you could have recorded the exact time everything changed. Suddenly death and decay descended upon the entire universe. Sickness, disease, cruelty, everything that makes this existence unbearable, all came as a result of Adam and Eve's act of disobedience. It truly was zero hour, the greatest moment of transformation in human history. The image of God in humanity plunged itself into the mud of sin. Death quickly followed.

All this seems a little extreme, especially in light of how small the first act of sin actually was. Pull an apple or a pear or a peach, or whatever the fruit might have been, off a tree and take a bite. Big deal. Stolen fruit. And it wasn't exactly stolen. God gave Adam and Eve the entire earth to do with as they pleased. So they took a bite? One bite. Surely God could forgive something so small, so insignificant. After all, he is the God of the second chance. Why couldn't he just wipe their slate clean and start over? Why does God make this such a big deal?

To appreciate the weight of the first sin, we need to see it from God's perspective. When Adam sinned, everyone sinned (see Romans 5:12-19). God had warned the couple that the penalty for disobedience was death, and even though they didn't keel over on the spot when they ate the fruit, they died. Spiritually. But they weren't the only ones affected. In some way I don't fully understand, you and I and every person were a part of Adam. The moment he took the fruit from his wife's hand, death spread to all of his descendants. As a result, human nature changed. The human heart became dark. We now have a heart that naturally enjoys doing what we know we shouldn't do. The Old Testament prophet Jeremiah put it this way: "The human heart is most deceitful and desperately wicked. Who really knows how bad it is? But I know! I, the LORD, search all hearts and examine secret motives" (17:9-10). That's a polite way of explaining why no one has to instruct us in the fine art of disobedience. Give us any rule, we'll break it. We start as soon as we're old enough to hear the word no, and we keep at it our whole lives. If, to paraphrase Pinocchio, "being bad weren't a lot of fun," police departments could sell their radar units to baseball scouts, and parents of toddlers would be much less frustrated.

Yet that's not the worst of it. The seed of every act of violence, every violation of another person, every cruel word, every war, every murder, all of it lay in that first act of disobedience. Sure, Adam and Eve ate a piece of fruit they weren't supposed to eat. Big deal. But if they had not, if when faced with temptation they had trusted God enough to do what he told them to do even though they didn't know why, the history of the human race would be different. The events of 9/11 would not have happened. The Holocaust, the killing fields of Cambodia, the terrors of Stalin, and the persecutions of Communist China—none of them would ever have occurred. Everything that makes us recoil against this world in disgust, everything that makes us long for a place where people get along and hearts don't break with grief and trees don't fall on cars, all of it is a direct result of the sin of Adam.

I guess one could still wonder if this sorry state that resulted from Adam and Eve's fall isn't God's fault. After all, if he hadn't planted the tree in the garden that started this mess, they wouldn't have disobeyed him. But the tree wasn't the problem; their lack of faith was. And once they stopped believing that God was who he said he was and when they doubted that he meant what he had said, they would have found some way to disobey him. The world we now live in is the end result. God did not speak into existence a world of drive-by shootings and random acts of violence. Human beings created this world for themselves.

God did, however, put into place a system whereby the logical consequences of our insubordination would build upon themselves. This spreads the blame for the cause of our pain and suffering far beyond the first man and woman. Every succeeding generation refined the first simple act of disobedience into an art form. In spite of countless efforts to clean up our own act, we've never changed. Wars and violence and cruelty against one another have marked all of human history. Sibling rivalry, jealousy, dysfunctional families, domestic violence, and murder go back to the very first family. Read through the first eleven chapters of the book of Genesis. The problems that plague us now plagued the human race then. Society didn't go to hell in a hand basket the day MTV came on the air. We as people all stand condemned before God as rebels who shove God away and then blame him when the mess we create for ourselves causes us heartache and pain.

This brings us to the great paradox of suffering. By our sin, the human race has created a world where pain and disease and death are the rule, not the exception. Yet when they strike us personally, we blame God and wonder why he doesn't do something about it. In the midst of it all stands God. He chooses to love us. I don't know why. If you were God and the crowning point of your creation thumbed its nose at you and did the very thing you warned it not to do, what would you do? Would you be quick to forgive if you knew this small act would soon erupt in violence and death and destruction? The journey from a fruit tree in paradise to unspeakable acts of terror is much shorter than any of us can imagine. God knew the risk even before he made the first man and woman, but he chose to make them—and love them even after they sinned—anyway. And he continues to love their children to this day. In fact, he loves us so much that he sacrificed his only Son to undo the effects of the Fall. Through Christ's death on the cross and his resurrection from the grave, you and I can find forgiveness and life. We don't suddenly become exempt from the lot of the rest of the human race, but the effects are reversed. Death no longer is the end but the beginning.

The title of this book asks the question with which the human race has always wrestled: How could a good God allow bad things to happen? But it isn't as though he has to intervene in the natural order of the world for bad things to strike us. Every day, tragedies occur. Floods wipe out homes in Texas, Japanese beetles devastate crops in Indiana, a child disappears from her bedroom in California. That's life in a fallen world. And no one, not even those who cling to Jesus by faith, are exempt. Job never thought all ten of his children would die in a sudden storm. People never think that the unthinkable will hit them personally. But it does. Life doesn't play favorites. Godly people lose their jobs. Parents who use the Bible as their guide have children who rebel. Tornadoes blow away church buildings as well as bars. Because of the lasting effects of Adam and Eve's sin, we live in a world where bad things happen to everybody. Earthly paradise no longer exists. Pain and heartache and grief eventually strike everyone who draws a breath, no matter how much we pray that they won't. That's the world we created, a world where everyone dies in the end, a world corrupted by the lasting effects of sin.

The great wonder of it all lies in God, who chooses to love us in spite of our sin. Although we separate ourselves from him by our disobedience, he promises never to leave us or forsake us (see Hebrews 13:5). Tragedy strikes, yet God works through all things to accomplish his greater purposes (see Romans 8:28). Why does suffering exist? As hard as it is to accept, suffering is one of the effects of sin, which means human beings ultimately brought it on themselves that day in the garden. Don't worry, however, because God already has done something about it. Something radical. Rather than end all suffering, he became flesh and shared it. By doing so he destroyed death's power to harm those who turn to him by faith.

Now, rather than shake an angry fist toward heaven blaming God for the raw deal he's given us, we must respond to his love. Jesus, God's only Son, died to pay the penalty you and I deserve for our sin. God did this because he loves us. Now he calls us to respond by turning away from our lives of sin and entrusting our lives to Christ. When we do, he forgives us completely and adopts us into his family. Believe me, this isn't a bargain we strike with God where we promise to follow him if he will promise to make our lives happy and complete. We don't have anything with which to bargain. God offers us real life, life worth living, eternal life that not only outlives the storms of our physical existence but also thrives in their midst. He offers all of this to us. We receive it by trusting in him completely.

Trusting God is the starting point for accepting whatever life throws at us. It also brings us full circle. The first man and woman's lack of faith in God started the chain of events that resulted in the world we cannot wait to escape. But God hasn't changed. He loves us in spite of ourselves. As we will see, nothing in this world can separate us from his love. When the unthinkable happens, this confidence will be put to the test. Through it all, we hear God calling us with the same simple message: "Trust me." Doing so would be a lot easier if we could figure God out, but we can't. He is God. We aren't. He commands us to trust him even when we cannot understand what he is doing or why he is doing it. If we cannot trust God, what hope do we have?

CHAPTER 3

THE DANGER OF LIVING WITH A GOD I CAN'T FIGURE OUT

The fad finally died down. Some saw it as a great spiritual move-ment, and maybe it was if little bracelets imprinted with four letters could spur people toward imitating the character of Christ. At least the cloth band encouraged the wearer to think, if only for a day, about how Jesus might respond to the situations we face. The effects seemed a little less than desired every time a high-profile ath-lete would take off on a profanity-laced tirade while the WWJD band hung around his wrist.

Hardly anyone wears them anymore. The hats and T-shirts gave way to the next big thing several next big things ago. For a while everyone asked the same question: What would Jesus do? When tempted, what would Jesus do? When you see a person in need, what would Jesus do? When you face a hard decision, what would Jesus do? The question implies we know enough of the character of the Savior to figure out how he would act if he lived in the twenty-first century with its unique pressures and temptations. At school or on the job or in the home, what would Jesus do if he traded places with you for a day?

The problem with the question is we don't know the answer. We may be able to figure out the really obvious situations. It is a safe bet Jesus wouldn't do drugs or cheat on his taxes. Beyond that our answers have as much of a chance of being wrong as right. That was what was confusing about Jesus when he walked this earth. He never did what anyone expected. The places he went, the people he chose to be around, the things he did, none of it fit the preconceived notions of what the Messiah would be. No one, not even those closest to him, expected him to die. The religious leaders rejected him because he didn't act very messianic. No Savior of the Jews would ever break the Sabbath with such impunity. He would never defile himself and allow unclean people to touch him. He would never claim equality with God, which is exactly what Jesus did when he called God his Father. What would the Messiah do? Certainly not what they watched Jesus do. That's why they put him to death as an impostor.

We face the same problem, not only when we look at the cloth band around our wrists but also when we try to figure out what God is doing in our lives at any precise moment. He seldom, if ever, does what we expect. But then again, he never did. The Bible is full of stories of the unexpected, not just the stories about Jesus. The first recorded words of God should catch us off guard. "Let there be light," he said (Genesis 1:3). Who but God would create light before making a light source? Who but God would create a world and fill it with plants before hanging the sun or the stars in the sky? After he looked at creation and called it very good, why would he allow Satan to come crawling into the Garden of Eden? Why did he allow Cain to live after he committed the first murder in human history? I can act all pious, I can act like I know the answers, but I don't. No one knows why God did what he did then or why he does what he does today. Just read the first fifteen chapters of the Bible. God always defies conventional wisdom. Honestly, did you see the ark coming as a way of preserving human history? Of course not. That's one of the reasons skeptics howl that the story can't be true. It doesn't fit into our preconceived notions of the way an all-powerful God would work.

Then there's the story of Abraham. In case you're unfamiliar with it, let me summarize it for you. God decides he wants to make himself known to the world. In fact, God decides he wants to bless all humanity. So what does he do? He chooses Abraham (a man no one's ever heard of), moves him to a dusty strip of land, and has him live in a tent the rest of his life. Then, nearly thirty-five years after Abraham and his wife are old enough to draw full Social Security benefits, God gives them one child. One. Yeah, that sounds like a real efficient way of getting the word out that you are the one true God who wants the whole world to know you personally. As if the plan wasn't strange enough, God tells Abraham to take his only son up on top of a mountain and sacrifice him there. What kind of plan is this? This is how God wants to make himself known to the entire world? It strikes me as absurd. The plan worked, but it took a couple thousand years. God is God and this is the best plan he can come up with? Why?

Every time we read the Bible, that same question hits us. The Lord works in mysterious ways, which is just a polite way of saying that God does some really strange things. He acts in ways that don't make sense to anyone but him. If that's how God worked in the Bible, what makes us think he'll act any differently in our day-to-day lives? I still try to figure out what he's up to when my life takes an unexpected turn. Worse yet, I find myself trying to anticipate his next move or trying to explain what he just did. I'm almost always wrong. I don't know what he is up to. I usually have no idea.

That's the real problem. We can't figure God out. We don't know what he is up to. We don't know why he does what he does. From our limited human perspective, God's actions too often don't make sense. The wise thing to do, the prudent course of action, would be to put a cork in our explanations and simply hang on tight to his hand, even when we're not sure his hand is there. But whoever said we like to do the wise thing? Most of us don't want to admit we can't figure God out. Instead we try to explain him away. And when we hear someone cry out that God isn't being fair or that life needs some major improvements, we step in with our best God talk and give that person all the answers.

That's what three of Job's friends did shortly after his life came apart.

Word of Job's demise spread quickly through the land of Uz. Apparently, many people found great delight in his tragedy. They weren't being exceptionally cruel, just human. How many of us would shed any tears if Donald Trump declared bankruptcy tomorrow? Before the tragedies, Job was more than a righteous man or a wealthy man. The Bible calls him the greatest man in all the ancient Near East. Conversations stopped when he walked by. People stared in awe. Old men stood out of respect when he entered a room. He had the final word in every dispute. Princes and city officials listened quietly to him and heeded his advice. Oppressed widows and orphans ran to him for help. Job fed the poor, defended the powerless, upheld justice. He fought for those who couldn't stand up for themselves. Even strangers received a fair trial when Job came around.

But all that changed the day Satan came before God and pointed an accusing finger at Job. No one on earth knew anything about this conversation. They couldn't hear God call Job "the finest man in all the earth" (Job 1:8). No one suspected that the tragedy that rained down on Job and his family had a divine purpose other than judgment. God wanted to prove that Job would fear him even if he had nothing to gain. Everyone in the grandstands of heaven understood this; no one on earth did. As disaster struck, it didn't take long for the hushed tones of respect Job once enjoyed to become mocking laughter. Everyone believed that Job finally got his, and they were glad. The man who was so quick to lecture others couldn't say anything when his life fell apart. The sudden turn of events convinced most people there had to be more to Job than anyone knew, a secret life of sin for which God now cursed him. Everyone stayed away from him. No one wanted to stand too close just in case God had a few more lightning bolts to throw Job's way.

Three men decided to risk it and go see their old friend. Eliphaz, Bildad, and Zophar went to Job to offer their comfort and support. When they found him they were shocked. He didn't look like the Job they remembered. His face was gaunt, his skin a sick reddish black from the boils covering him from head to toe. Pus oozed and formed a disgusting paste when mixed with the ashes with which Job covered himself as a sign of mourning. Just the sight of him made them break down in tears. I don't know what Eliphaz, Bildad, and Zophar planned to say to Job when they arrived. Whatever it was stuck in their throats. None of them could say a word. They simply sat down next to him and remained silent for seven days.

Then Job spoke up and said that God was ultimately responsible for everything that happened. Hatred didn't well up in his voice. He didn't shake a fist at heaven and accuse God through clenched teeth. His three friends would have preferred such an outburst. What he did was even worse: Job held on to his integrity. He claimed to be the innocent victim of God's wrath. "All God's terrors are arrayed against me," he said.[1] "What I've always feared has now happened. I wish I'd never been born," he moaned. All Job wanted to know was why. Why was this happening? If only God would turn his back on Job and leave him alone, that would be better than being the target of his poison darts. "God did this, and I don't know why," he cried. "Why does God give life to those he plans to subject to a life of distress? It doesn't make any sense to me, and God wouldn't answer me even if I could gain an audience with him." You can sense the resignation in his voice. "Who can argue with God?" he asked. "He can do anything he wants, and no one can stop him or rebuke him. God did this and I don't know why."

Eliphaz was the first to answer. He couldn't get the words out fast enough. "Will you be patient and let me say a word? For who could keep from speaking out?" (Job 4:2). That's just another way of saying, "Shut up, you ignorant blabbermouth, and let me tell you what's really going on." Eliphaz reminded Job that God wouldn't do the things he charged him with. Harm the innocent? Impossible. That's not the way God works. "Tell me, Job," Eliphaz wanted to know, "when were the upright ever destroyed? Don't you know that those who plow evil and sow trouble always reap it?"[2] "God's not the one to blame for these problems. Sure, he sent this calamity, but only because YOU DESERVED IT!" I can only imagine how much better that made Job feel. And, yes, I'm being sarcastic.

Bildad and Zophar followed suit. Job's comforters became his accusers. They couldn't help themselves. Job impugned God's honor, and they had to rise to defend it. All of their speeches, everything they said that fills the book of Job, came down to this: God blesses the righteous and strikes down the wicked. If God struck Job, he must have deserved it. A good God would never do anything to harm someone he loves. So much for sympathizing and comforting. They glanced down at their WWGD bracelets and concluded: God wouldn't do this. Ever. And Job kept saying the same thing in response: I don't know why he did this, but he did.

Job's friends thought they had God figured out, and Job may have thought the same thing before his ten children died and his health failed. The safe God, the loving God, the God who always blesses the righteous and punishes the wicked, was either acting out of character or Job was not the righteous man everyone had been led to believe. Job's friends couldn't conceive that the first option could be true. It had to be the latter. They had no choice. They had to believe it. Sitting with Job for seven days, looking around at the destruction, feeling the depth of his grief and sorrow scared them. Job said it himself: "You have seen my calamity, and you are afraid" (Job 6:21). The fear that swept over them did not come from the raiding Sabeans or the clouds that rolled overhead. No, Eliphaz, Bildad, and Zophar came face-to-face with a God who scared them to death. If God would strike Job, a righteous and holy man who offered sacrifices for his children just in case they might have sinned, what might he do to them? They could either cower in fear or cling to the more palatable God they'd always hoped was true.

At the end of the book, God finally tells Job's friends they are wrong. He goes on to tell Job to pray for them. I always wonder what ran through their minds at this point. Did the sound of distant thunder send them scrambling? Did they move closer to the safety and security of a walled city? But where could they go to hide from God? They found themselves in a very uncomfortable position. The three of them defended God's honor only to be rebuked by God himself. "The Almighty would never do such a thing," they repeated over and over only to hear God whisper, "Oh, but I did."

Did he? And if he did, was God acting out of character? The trouble in reading the book of Job is the wrong people sound right and the hero of the book sounds so wrong. Job attributed to God acts that appear evil. Even after reading the story, we cannot believe he is right. I got a taste of this when I told a friend what this book was about. The moment the words "Should we accept good things from God and not bad?" came out of my mouth, he immediately shot back, "But God doesn't send bad things. He allows them to happen." My friend went on to point out how Satan was the real culprit in the book of Job. God allowed Satan to do bad things, but he himself was not responsible. Only good gifts come from God, never anything bad. My friend wasn't telling me anything I hadn't already heard a million times. Another friend gave me another version of the same argument when the tree fell on Stan's car. Like Eliphaz, both felt compelled to defend God's honor.

In their zeal to defend God, my friends actually disrespected him. They, like many of us, tried to draw a line of distinction between God's permissive will and his causative will. What would God do? He wouldn't do evil. Sometimes he allows evil to exist and work to serve his greater purposes, but he doesn't cause it. That sounds great. But if I answer the door and find a police officer and the fire department chaplain standing there to break the news to me that my son died in a car wreck, the distinction between the different types of God's will is not going to lessen the pain I feel. Neither will all of the sweet-sounding little sayings that people offer to try to make hurting people feel better, sayings that also help God escape culpability. I nearly throw up every time I hear someone say something like, "God must have needed him in heaven more than we need him here on earth." If you tell me God didn't do this, he only allowed it to happen, does that lessen the anger I feel toward God or the fear that grips me at the thought of him?

And fear does grip me because I know acts that appear on a human level to be evil or unjust are not out of character for the God of the Bible. The eighth chapter of Romans is a chapter everyone who wants a safe, clean, easy-to-understand God needs to avoid at all costs. In it Paul expands on God's words to Moses: "I will show mercy to anyone I choose, and I will show compassion to anyone I choose" (Exodus 33:19). Paul chooses two Old Testament examples to show how God will do whatever he wants to whomever he wants. The first is Isaac and his two sons. Isaac's wife, Rebekah, bore twin sons, Esau and Jacob. Before either was born, God made up his mind to love Jacob and reject Esau. Nothing either of them did during their lives changed God's mind. Jacob was a swindler, tricking his brother out of his birthright and his father's blessings. Esau, although his father's favorite, comes across as a tragic character, desperately seeking the blessing that will never be his. And none of this matters to God. "I loved Jacob, but I rejected Esau," God declares in Romans 9:13.

Paul's second example is Pharaoh. We all remember Pharaoh as the evil king of Egypt who refused to set the children of Israel free. Moses came before him and performed miracle after miracle while asking for freedom for the slaves. Yet each miracle only caused Pharaoh's heart to grow a little colder, a little harder, and he refused to budge. Instead of setting the slaves free he increased their misery, forcing them to make bricks without straw. It is hard to feel much sympathy for a ruthless, cold-blooded villain like Pharaoh — that is until we read his story in the first twelve chapters of Exodus. The Bible clearly says that God hardened Pharaoh's heart (see Exodus 9:12; 10:1,20,27; 11:10). Paul recounts the story and God's words to Pharaoh: "I have appointed you for the very purpose of displaying my power in you, and so that my fame might spread throughout the earth" (Romans 9:17). Then Paul adds, "So you see, God shows mercy to some just because he wants to, and he chooses to make some people refuse to listen. Well then, you might say, 'Why does God blame people for not listening. Haven't they simply done what he made them do?' No, don't say that. Who are you, a mere human being, to criticize God?" (Romans 9:18-20).

Was God unfair to Esau or Pharaoh? According to Paul we don't even have the right to ask the question. Since God is God, he can do anything and everything he wants. He is the potter. He has the right to use one lump of clay to make a beautiful pot and another for a trash can, and neither the pot nor the trash can has any right to complain. God is God. He will do whatever he desires. And, if it sounds more palatable to you, he will allow whatever he decides to allow, even if it causes us pain and trouble and heartache. Just or unjust, fair or unfair, good or bad, whatever it may look like to us doesn't really matter. God is God. He will do what he wants, and none of us will ever be able to fully figure out why or how.

As I said a moment ago, the thought of a God I cannot figure out doing whatever he wants leaves me a little frightened. I feel as though I am suddenly swinging without a net. I know that anything may well happen to me. When my daughters jump into a car and go off to a movie together, I have no guarantee they will come home safely. Nor do I have any guarantees that I will still have a job tomorrow or that a fire will not strike during the night and burn down my house. This isn't Murphy's Law. Anything bad will not necessarily happen, but it also isn't Eliphaz's law, where bad things happen only to bad people. I don't know what God will do next. I'm not sure what he is up to right now, as he never feels compelled to explain himself to me.

However, there is one thing he does say. He tells us to trust him enough to believe he knows what he is doing. Proverbs 3:5 puts it this way: "Trust in the LORD with all your heart; do not depend on your own understanding." When God's actions don't make sense, trust him. When the windows of heaven seem to be open extra wide and life can't get any better, trust him. When the bottom falls out and life turns hard, trust him. Good times and bad, happy and sad, trust him. When I try to explain God or reduce him to neat little formulas, I show a lack of faith.

What will God do? I have no idea, but I do know this: God is God. His wisdom knows no end. He isn't making things up on the fly. He knows what he is doing. Now I must trust him enough to entrust my life to him even when I would rather not.

CHAPTER 4

THIS ISN'T WHAT I SIGNED UP FOR

One of the early forms of witness wear, the clothes that make a statement for God, played on an old Coca-Cola campaign and said, "Things Go Better with Jesus." Or maybe it was "with God." I can't recall, even though I think I had one back when I attended youth camps as a camper rather than an over-the-hill counselor. It didn't take much courage to have on witness wear at a church camp. Everywhere you turned, someone's shirt said something like, "Property of Jesus Christ" or "Jesus" in the middle of the Pepsi logo or, my personal favorite, "If You Think God Is Far Away, Guess Who Moved?" The last one had a cartoon of a little man dragging his house behind his car. Wearing the shirts to school was another matter entirely. Walking through the halls of Moore High School sporting a shirt that said anything about God was a real test of faith—and a way to witness. That's why I chose shirts with positive messages. I wanted to let people know that life would be better with Jesus, and a couple of years later, when my life stopped measuring up to the message I once conveyed, I hoped they had a short memory.

Since wandering away from God as a seventeen-year-old and later coming back to him, I have come to believe that life really is better with Jesus. That's the message I want to get out. We all do. Why else would the little booklets we hand out to introduce people to Jesus have titles like "Steps to Peace with God" or "How to Have a Full and Meaningful Life" or "The Road to Hope"? No one ever hands out tracts with titles like "Trust God and Watch Your Life Go into the Toilet" or "Give God Control and He'll Drive You over a Cliff." The quality of our lives is supposed to improve when we follow Christ by faith. After all, Jesus himself said, "The thief's purpose is to steal and kill and destroy. My purpose is to give life in all its fullness" (John 10:10). A full life. A meaningful life. That's what we expect from God.

High expectations do not presume upon God. Throughout the Bible, God promises to give his best to those who love him. He gave before there were people to ask for anything from him. In the beginning, before corruption began to defile creation, before he created people, God planted a garden paradise to be the special home of the first man and woman. A few chapters later when he called Abraham to follow him, God gave this promise: "I will cause you to become the father of a great nation. I will bless you and make you famous, and I will make you a blessing to others. I will bless those who bless you and curse those who curse you. All the families of the earth will be blessed through you" (Genesis 12:2-3). Did you hear what God said? "I will bless you. . . . I will make you a blessing. . . . All the families on the earth will be blessed through you." God repeated this promise several times to Abraham and renewed the covenant with Abraham's son Isaac and grandson Jacob.

A few hundred years later, the descendants of Abraham had indeed become a great nation, albeit a nation of slaves. God set them free, carried them through the desert, and gave them the land he promised to

Abraham. Before they crossed the Jordan River to start the process of conquering the land, God spoke again through the prophet Moses:

> If you listen to these regulations and obey them faithfully, the LORD your God will keep his covenant of unfailing love with you, as he solemnly promised your ancestors. He will love you and bless you and make you into a great nation. He will give you many children and give fertility to your land and your animals. When you arrive in the land he swore to give your ancestors, you will have large crops of grain, grapes, and olives, and great herds of cattle, sheep, and goats. You will be blessed above all the nations of the earth. None of your men or women will be childless, and all your livestock will bear young. And the LORD will protect you from all sickness. He will not let you suffer from the terrible diseases you knew in Egypt, but he will bring them all on your enemies! (Deuteronomy 7:12-15)

Again, God used the B-word, *blessing*. This time he gets very specific. In this land they had never seen, a land God had promised to give them four hundred years earlier, they would have everything they ever needed. If they would simply obey God, the nation of Israel would become the envy of the world. As if this wasn't enough, God instructed the priests to announce the following blessing over his people time and time again:

> May the LORD bless you
> and protect you.
> May the LORD smile on you
> and be gracious to you.

May the LORD show you his favor
  and give you his peace.

This is how Aaron and his sons will designate
the Israelites as my people, and I myself will bless
them. (Numbers 6:24-27)

Call it a hunch, but I think God's blessing you and protecting you and smiling on you means your life will see a noticeable improvement. The children of Israel certainly did. God kept his promise and gave them a land that flowed with milk and honey. Gave it to them. Sure, they had to fight some battles to take possession of it, but God fought for them. When Abraham's descendants came upon one city beyond their ability to conquer, God told them to march around it every day for a week. On the eighth day, they were to shout and blow trumpets and watch God knock the walls down. They did and he did (see Joshua 6). It took some time, but they finally took possession of the land, complete with wells they didn't dig and vineyards and orchards they didn't plant. Vineyards and orchards may not sound like much to us today in comparison to the kind of comforts the average American enjoys, but back then they were really something.

A few centuries later, the nation reached the pinnacle of God's blessings. Under the leadership of King Solomon, a man God hand-selected as king, Israel achieved a level of success we can relate to. Gold became so common that silver lost its value. Everyone's pockets jingled with cash, and their barns were full of horses and their silos overflowed with grain. Surrounding countries sent gifts and paid tribute to Israel's king. Peace ruled the land. In the center of it all sat the Lord's temple, the place where he made his presence known in a physical way to his people (see 1 Kings 3–10). "Things Go Better with God" T-shirts probably would have been hot sellers if anyone had gone to the trouble of inventing the T-shirt. God promised to bless his people, and he did.

Yet a sad irony resounds throughout the pages of the Bible. Almost all who experienced a life filled with material blessings, the best this world has to offer, soon found themselves drifting away from God. Adam and Eve lived in paradise, but they threw it away and did not remain obedient to the one command God gave them. The children of Israel abandoned the Lord for a host of strange idols one generation after settling in the land that flowed with milk and honey. Apparently, having every physical need met wasn't all it was cracked up to be. Solomon himself, the wisest man who ever lived — a man to whom God personally appeared twice, the man who built the temple in Jerusalem, a man whose annual income exceeded six hundred tons of gold — built shrines to false gods in his old age. The pattern repeats itself throughout the Old Testament. Good times often lead to weaker faith, compromised commitment, and, ultimately, turning away from God.

Which brings us back to Job and a God we can't figure out. The day Job lost everything — his flocks and herds, his servants, and all his worldly wealth, even his health — he asked his wife, "Should we accept good things from God and not bad?" Throughout most of his adult life, Job enjoyed good things from God. That doesn't mean he never suffered prior to this point, but the book of Job does not give us those details. In a moment everything changed. Yet nothing changed. The Lord gave. The Lord took away. "Praise the name of the Lord," Job said (see Job 1:21). God gave good stuff. Now he gives bad. Same God. *How can I accept one and not the other?* Job wanted to know. He sounds like a man reciting wedding vows: "For better or worse, for richer or poorer, in sickness and in health." Good or bad, we can't accept one without the other.

Yet this isn't what we expect, or want, from God. We can accept that married life will be full of ups and downs. After all, marriage is the joining of two imperfect people living in an imperfect world. But that doesn't describe God. Not only is he good and perfect, he also possesses the power to do anything and everything he decides to do. Hard times shouldn't be a part of the equation, and if they are, there must be more than one Bible with competing promises. Raiding Sabeans killing all your servants and riding off with your flocks doesn't sound much like a life of blessing. Fire falling from heaven appears to contradict "You will be blessed above all the nations of the earth" (Deuteronomy 7:14). No wonder Job's friends were so convinced Job must have done something horrible to anger God. How else can you reconcile all God promises to those who love him with a windstorm blowing down houses, killing everyone inside?

The answer lies in looking beyond the flocks and herds to see the true nature of God's blessings. The pattern of the Old Testament shows how material blessings never brought about greater intimacy with God. In fact, the opposite nearly always resulted. In the Old Testament, the Israelites forgot about God when their barns were full and their pockets jingled. But when life took a serious turn for the worse, they fell on their faces before him and pleaded for him to return to them.

Job stands out as the exception to the rule. He is one of the few consistently wealthy people in the Bible whose heart stayed fast upon God. And that was the nature of the wager between God and Satan. Satan had accused God of buying Job's devotion. But Job's resolution to continue believing in God even though everything around him screamed to do the opposite displayed God's greatness and silenced his critic—something material blessings could never do.

When bad things rained down upon Job, God hadn't forgotten him. The opposite was the case. In the moment of tragedy, God's full and undivided attention focused upon the one he described as the greatest man of the east. Job thought his prayers bounced off the ceiling unheard. He could not understand the silence from heaven.

Yet the silence did not mean that God's blessings were suddenly taken away. No, God had something much greater in mind for his servant. Through his nightmare, Job would now bring glory to God not just on earth but throughout heaven as well.

Job's trust didn't waver because he understood that God's greatest blessings have nothing to do with this world of time. Ephesians 1:3 tells us that in Christ, God has "blessed us with every spiritual blessing in the heavenly realms." A land flowing with milk and honey sounds like small potatoes in comparison. Every spiritual blessing means more than cows having calves once a year or grapevines bearing a bumper crop. The first chapter of Ephesians goes on to tell us how God promises to adopt us into his family, forgive our every failure, grant us peace in a chaotic world, and shower us with his presence every day, even when he feels far away. Job looked ahead to the coming of God's Messiah, just as we look forward to his return, but the principles are the same for both scenarios. God's greatest blessings give us something far better than physical stuff that does not last.

We read all of this, and somewhere in the back of our minds it registers, "God's blessings deal with eternity and his glory, not with something as fleeting and temporary as material goods." Yet when trouble strikes us, we have trouble equating Job's experience with our own lives. *Where are the blessings?* we wonder. *Why is God doing this to me? Doesn't he love me?* We must remember that, as hard as it is to fathom, neither good times nor bad serve as an accurate barometer of God or his faithfulness. Trouble does not mean he has taken his blessings away. All the best that heaven can offer still belongs to us. Because these are blessings from heaven, they don't necessarily have anything to do with houses and land and happiness. Having good times doesn't mean God loves us more, and having bad times doesn't mean he loves us less. As the writer of Ecclesiastes said, "Enjoy prosperity while you can. But when hard times strike, realize that both come from God. That way you will realize that nothing is certain in this life" (7:14).

We may expect God to give us a happier, more fulfilling life, a life of purpose and happy endings, but that doesn't mean we will experience that life in the way we expect. Yes, God promised the children of Israel a land where the rain always fell and cows always gave milk and the sheep frolicked on green hills. But the New Testament tells us that God has something better in store for us. God never promises to make us happy in a Hollywood sitcom kind of way. In fact, in the Sermon on the Mount, Jesus said that those who experience the greatest blessing from God are those who are poor and hungry and persecuted for the sake of righteousness. The term translated *blessing* could also be translated *happy*. The first few lines of the Sermon on the Mount could be translated, "Happy are the poor in spirit, happy are those who mourn, happy are the meek, happy are you when people insult you and persecute you and falsely say all kinds of evil against you because of me" (see Matthew 5:3-11). Jesus goes on to say that his blessings lie in something that goes beyond this life. The poor in spirit possess the kingdom of heaven, those who mourn will be comforted, the meek will inherit the earth, and those who are persecuted for the sake of Christ will receive a great reward in heaven. But that doesn't necessarily translate into a happier, more fulfilling life right now.

God's promise to bless us has nothing to do with a life of comfort or ease or success. If it did, Adam and Eve never would have left the garden, and Solomon wouldn't have spent the last few years of his life nailing together shrines to Molech. God's greatest blessing, the greatest gift he gives us, is the gift of himself. That's it. Heaven is not about streets of gold but about God. Anything good we receive in this life is simply icing on the cake.

Every spiritual blessing in the heavenly realms now belongs to those who know Christ. The blessings are ours, even when they take on surprising forms.

CHAPTER 5

WHAT I ALWAYS FEARED

"What I always feared has happened to me," Job cried out to no one in particular. "What I dreaded has come to be." He paused and scratched at the scabs on his arm. His eyes looked distant, all the emotion drained from his face. "I have no peace," he muttered, "no quietness. I have no rest; instead, only trouble comes" (Job 3:25-26). If Eliphaz, Bildad, and Zophar hadn't chimed in, those might have been his last words. What more could he say? His worst-case scenarios all came true. The one worry with the power to wake him up in the middle of the night in a cold sweat was now his day-to-day life. You can hear him running the white flag up the pole. He might as well say he gives up. All he has left to do is lie down and wait for death to come. Life can't get any worse.

Here's what I find odd about Job's words. He never tells us what his greatest fear was. Maybe he thought it was so obvious he didn't need to explain it. Perhaps he thought that every parent could figure it out. I'm a parent. Like Job, I have three daughters. What could possibly be worse than losing one or all of them? If I stop and listen, I can hear the servant's message to Job: "The house collapsed, and all your children are dead." I do my best to chase such thoughts away, but deep down I know the same fate could hit my family. And yours.

We would rather lose everything else, even our own lives. Job was a father. Surely he, too, feared losing his children.

Or maybe he dreaded the thought of becoming penniless. Job had everything he could possibly desire. His seven thousand sheep, three thousand camels, five hundred teams of oxen, and five hundred female donkeys made him the Bill Gates of his day. He was the richest person in that part of the world. Imagine waking up one morning and finding it was all gone. The sheep. The camels. The oxen. All of it gone. My retirement account lost one fourth of its value in a year and a half. I thought that was pretty bad. To lose everything? How much worse could life become? Where would you live? What would you eat? How could you survive? Job must have been afraid of losing all his possessions.

Or his health. Satan said, "A man will give up everything he has to save his life" (Job 2:4), and he wasn't far from the truth. We all fear contracting some horrible disease. I once knew a guy who drank wheatgrass juice every day because he heard it warded off cancer (and if you've never tried wheatgrass juice, suffice it to say you have to be pretty scared of cancer to choke it down). When Job lost everything but his health, he sat down in mourning and continued to praise the Lord's name. One chapter later, we find him cursing the day of his birth. Perhaps the boils covering his body finally took their toll. Job didn't know if he would survive. As far as he knew, death could come at any moment. Scraping arms and legs with a broken piece of pottery, enduring the pain day after day after day, surely Job now lived through his greatest nightmare.

Again, there's something odd about Job's words. If he feared losing his children or his wealth or his health, wouldn't he mention them somewhere in the rest of the book? But he never does. Job never calls God unfair for afflicting him with scabs. He never asks why his children had to die. Later in the book, Job talks about the disgrace heaped on his head as he walks through the city, but he never mourns the loss of his possessions. If Job's fear of all fears, the nightmare that caused him to break out in a cold sweat, consisted of losing his family or his wealth or his health, or even the combination of the three, one or all would constantly rise up as the focal point of his complaints against God. Since they don't, we have to ask again, *What was Job so afraid of?*

After reading through all forty-two chapters of Job, I think the answer is obvious: God. Job was afraid of God. All his life he worried that God would turn against him. Remember, Job didn't have sixty-six books of the Bible to console him. Most scholars think he lived even before Moses penned Genesis. Everything Job knew about God had been handed down to him by previous generations. Although Job served God wholeheartedly, deep in his heart lay the fear that God would reject him. Now he had. "Tell me, what have I done?" Job shouted toward heaven. "Show me my rebellion and my sin. Why do you turn away from me? Why do you consider me your enemy?" (Job 13:23-24).

More than losing his children, more than losing his health or his wealth, Job feared God's turning his back on him. All his life, Job did everything in his power to keep that from happening. He prayed and sacrificed and expressed his devotion to God. But he didn't stop there. Job walked his talk. If a beautiful woman walked by, he averted his eyes rather than gawk and lust. He worked to be content with what he had, and he generously shared with those in need. Even though he was rich, he never trusted in his possessions for security. He depended on God alone. No one had to wonder about what he said. Job's word was like gold. He was in every way a person of integrity. Job wasn't trying to buy God's favor; he did all of this because he loved God.

Suddenly, from Job's perspective, it was over. God had unilaterally ended their relationship. Job didn't know why. For the first time in his life he felt very, very alone. God was nowhere to be found. "I go east," Job complained, "but he is not there. I go west, but I cannot find him. I do not see him in the north, for he is hidden. I turn to the south, but I cannot find him" (Job 23:8-9). God never spoke. He offered no comfort, no reassurance from the Holy Spirit—only distant silence. God had turned his back on Job.

Not only had God turned away from Job, but Eliphaz, Bildad, and Zophar kept telling Job that God was angry with him. The blessings Job once enjoyed looked like a cruel joke, as though God had lured him in only to knock him down. "You gave me life and showed me your unfailing love," Job called out to God. "My life was preserved by your care. Yet your real motive—I know this was your intent—was to watch me, and if I sinned, you would not forgive my iniquity." You pulled me in, Job said, only to destroy me. "If I am guilty, too bad for me. And if I am innocent, I am filled with shame and misery so that I can't hold my head high. And if I hold my head high, you hunt me like a lion and display your awesome power against me" (Job 10:12-16). All his life Job lived with the fear that God might turn against him. Now that he had, what hope did Job have?

"If God is for us, who can ever be against us?" Paul wrote in Romans 8:31. Yet where can we run when God appears to turn against us? I know you're thinking that God would never turn against one of his children. But haven't you ever asked yourself, *What if he does?* We take so much for granted from God. We automatically assume that our every need troubles him as much as it troubles us. We know he owns the cattle on a thousand hills. Few of us are shy about asking him to sell a few to come to our aid. Right now the biggest "need" in the Tabb household is air-conditioning. We recently moved into a one-hundred-year-old house that lacks central air. Never mind that Indiana summer temperatures rarely climb into the nineties. All of us at one time or another have groaned about the heat and humidity. As soon as God provides the funds to put it in, we'll have a new condensing unit sitting right outside my office window. As much as I long for some relief from the heat, in my honest moments I ask myself why God should provide me with air-conditioning or three square meals a day or more than one set of clothes to wear. Why should I receive more than believers on the other side of the globe who are glad when they eat one meal a day, who enjoy meat only on special occasions, people who live with one or two sets of clothes and die before their fiftieth birthday? Usually I push such thoughts out of my mind. God will come through for me. He always has. I assume he always will.

What if he doesn't? Jesus told the rich young ruler to give away everything he owned. The man refused because he owned a lot of stuff. I own a lot of stuff. If right now, at this moment, God told me to sell everything I own, I don't know if I could do it. Could you? Would you sell your house and your car and your computer and everything else, give the money to the poor, and become homeless and penniless for Christ? Why should God continue to bless my life when I put things before him? Why wouldn't God strike me down for my materialism or my lack of compassion? My brothers and sisters in Christ in other parts of the world daily give their lives for the cause of Christ. Today in the Sudan, tens of thousands of believers suffer in slavery. For the children, slavery is only the beginning of their problems. Muslim capturers routinely rape both young boys and girls.[1] Why should God be on my side while I do nothing to fight for justice on their behalf?

Those of us privileged enough to live in a land with religious freedom tend to marginalize God. We want a God in a box, a deity we can let out when life gets rough. Yet Jesus laid out a radical way of life for his disciples. I'm not sure I qualify. Radical? I march for life every fall with the local crisis pregnancy center. Isn't that enough? Somehow I don't think it is. Why then if I fail to live on the cutting edge of discipleship, if my life doesn't display the fanatical devotion to Christ of the apostles, would I assume God is for me? No one could blame him, least of all me, if he changed his mind and placed me squarely in the crosshairs of his wrath.

This fear gripped Job, and one day it appeared to become reality. From a purely human perspective, God appeared to turn against him. His flocks and herds gone, his children dead, and oozing sores covering him from head to toe, Job's life didn't exactly look like a life God was blessing. Trying to go about a semi-normal life didn't help. Worthless people, the sort of characters to whom Job wouldn't even entrust his sheepdogs, now walked up to him and spit in his face. He couldn't fight back. What if he deserved it? Then there were the rumors. His comforters told him how horrible he must be for God to be so angry with him. Everyone around him must have thought the same thing. Even Job had to wonder.

As Job looked back over his life, he came face-to-face with an even more troubling possibility. He knew his integrity. No matter what his friends might say, he could not admit he was guilty of sins he hadn't committed. God wasn't punishing him. Job was absolutely certain of that, which only left one other possibility: Apparently, God had turned against Job for no reason whatsoever. The Almighty must not be as loving and compassionate as Job thought. Job concluded that watching righteous people suffer must give the Lord some sort of pleasure. C. S. Lewis wondered the same thing when he felt unbearable grief: "The conclusion I dread is not 'So there's no God after all,' but 'So this is what God's really like. Deceive yourself no longer.'"[2]

So this is what God is really like. Cruel, heartless, someone who sends plagues on good people while allowing scoundrels to live without a care; this is what God is really like. Job trembled at the thought. The idea goes against everything we think we know about God. When times are good, no one ever entertains the possibility that God might be cruel. But when suffering strikes, we can't help but think it. *So this is what God is really like,* we fear. No one says it out loud. All our lives we hear that God is loving and merciful and kind. But what if he's cruel? What if he will turn against us in the hour we need him most? Could this be what God is really like? Have we deceived ourselves into thinking differently?

"I've thought that," my best friend Chris told me in a hushed tone when I told him about this chapter. "I've wondered that very thing." Chris never considered the possibility before the character attacks began. At the time of this writing, a small group of people are trying to ruin his reputation and destroy his career. He doesn't know how the story will end, but it probably won't end well. These stories never do. His wife can't sleep. Their six children alternate between anger and sadness. None of them even knows if they'll still have a house six months from now. In his quiet moments, Chris wonders if God has turned against him. "I wonder what I might have done," he told me as we talked for an hour yesterday. "God feels closer than ever before," Chris said, "but it is different. He feels . . . frightening."

And he is. God is very frightening, more than words can describe.

I know at this point I need to reassure all of us that our God does not turn against his children, but I can't bring myself to say it—not yet at least. Hearing how much God loves us and cares for us and will never forsake us doesn't alleviate the thoughts that run through our minds when our suffering reaches a threshold we never thought we could stand. There comes a point in the midst of every crisis when we think, *So this is what God is really like. Deceive yourself no longer. The one I thought was behind me now stands on the other side of the aisle. My defender has become my accuser. My hope is now my dread.* If these thoughts have never crossed your mind, count yourself fortunate. Don't be surprised if they do. Suffering offers no limit to the despair it unleashes.

We will get to the reassurances of God's unfailing love later. I want to look deeper into this fear before I run away from it as fast as my legs will carry me. Job didn't have any choice but to stare his fears in the face. He tried running away, but he had nowhere to go. Finally he stood toe-to-toe with the dread that overwhelmed him and wrote, "This is what [God] says to all humanity: 'The fear of the Lord is true wisdom; to forsake evil is real understanding'" (Job 28:28). The phrase "the fear of the Lord" takes on a completely different meaning in light of the rest of Job's laments. He doesn't use the term as a synonym for respect or as a loose equivalent of faith. Sit down sometime and read all of Job's other speeches. He found God absolutely terrifying. And that's where wisdom begins.

You may howl in protest. "God isn't like this," you say. "He walks with me and he talks with me and he tells me I am his own. Frightening? Maybe to unbelievers, but not to those who know and love him. Jesus is our very best friend." I heard a man on an international Christian network speak of seeing God in his mirror every morning as he shaves. The guy didn't drop his razor in fear. Far from it. Every day he carries on a conversation with God as easily as he talks over his fence to his next-door neighbor. Terrifying? That's not the picture of God with which we're most familiar.

Yet it is exactly the portrayal of God we find throughout the Bible. When the children of Israel heard the voice of God thundering from Mount Sinai, they pleaded with Moses to keep him away from them. Isaiah saw the Lord in a vision and fell on his face as though dead. When Jesus calmed a storm while sailing across the Sea of Galilee with his disciples, they backed away and shook with fear. A team of Roman soldiers fell to the ground, paralyzed with fear, at the sight of the angel who rolled away the stone from Christ's tomb.

Imagine their reaction if they had actually seen Jesus alive again. John, one of the disciples closest to Jesus, saw the Lord in his resurrected power and fell before him in fear. To fear the Lord means more than respect or obedience. Fear means fear, knee-knocking, tongue-sticking-to-the-roof-of-the-mouth, palm-sweating fear — the same fear that gripped Job. And this fear is the beginning of wisdom.

Suffering strips everything to its bare essentials, including our understanding of God. All the candy-coated clichés fall by the wayside. Pithy little sayings and unrealistic concepts of God can't bear up under suffering's weight. Through pain God opens our eyes to see him in his awful power and majesty. As Chris told me, "God feels closer than ever, and I find him frightening." Job said the same thing: "No wonder I am so terrified in his presence. When I think of it, terror grips me. God has made my heart faint; the Almighty has terrified me" (Job 23:15-16).

Fear grips us, for not only do we see God for who he really is, we see our true selves as well. The moment leaves us naked before God with nowhere to run, no place to hide. We become painfully aware of our utter sinfulness. Job expressed what we all feel as his eyes opened to God:

> My ears had heard of you
>> but now my eyes have seen you.
> Therefore I despise myself
>> and repent in dust and ashes. (Job 42:5-6, NIV)

Suffering makes us all too aware that God owes us nothing. He promises to do good things for us, yet he is under no obligation to do anything for us beyond what our sin warrants. Anything good that comes our way, from a cool rain on a hot summer afternoon to the beating of our hearts seventy times a minute, all comes from God's grace. He owes us nothing. We deserve judgment.

This almost appears to be a contradiction. The previous chapter talked of how God has blessed us with all the blessings heaven can hold. Now I turn around and tell you that you and I don't deserve anything from God. It's not a contradiction. We don't *deserve* that which God has done for us. The moment we start thinking we do, we immediately start complaining about the raw deal God has given us.

The cries of Job, the honest, gut-wrenching laments, come from a deep fear of God. We long for answers. Our hearts and spirits lie completely broken. Distance from God drives us to our knees. We cry out, not for restored fortunes but restored fellowship. With Christ we can face anything. Without him we're left without any hope. The fear that we might be on our own drives us to cry out to him. We don't just want God's comfort; we need him. Desperately.

Job doesn't sound very heroic. That's all right. I have trouble relating to heroes who perform superhuman feats. But I can relate to someone whose fear of God drives him ever closer to the one he fears. Only there can I come close to being able to trust God through both the good times and the bad.

CHAPTER 6

TRUSTING GOD WHEN THE HOPE OF HEAVEN IS ALL YOU HAVE (OR WANT)

D on Holt lived a double life. And he did it better than anyone I've ever met.

I first met Don when a prison ministry volunteer leaned over to me and whispered, "See that guy over there?" and pointed across the room at a man who looked like he didn't have a care in the world. Relaxed, glasses hanging around his neck on a string, laughing with those around him, nothing about Don Holt made him appear any different from the other 150 volunteers who gave up this weekend to go into a prison with the Bill Glass Prison Ministry team. "He once had a five-hundred-year prison sentence," the man continued. I did a double take. Five hundred years? I wondered how many people he had to kill to get five hundred years. And then a shudder shot down my spine. The five-hundred-year guy wasn't one of the inmates we came to tell about Jesus. He came from the outside with us. I made a mental note to keep my distance.

But I couldn't. God kept throwing the two of us together. I managed to avoid Don during the three-day Weekend of Champions, but then I opened my big mouth and volunteered to come back once a week for the next six weeks to do follow-up. Guess who else volunteered? He also volunteered to pick me up at my house and drive us over to the prison together. A few months later, he started attending the church I served. His brother bought a house three doors down from my mother. I finally got the hint from God. Don Holt was a man I needed to get to know. What I found was a man unlike any person I knew. He lived two lives, and he did it quite well.

Don needed two lives because he had made such a mess of his first. Somewhere around the time I was born, Don did a little after-hours shopping at a drugstore. Since no one was on duty, he let himself in and helped himself to all the drugs he could find. A post office was right next door, and Don thought, *Since I'm already here I might as well make my trip worth while.* The police pulled up while he dug through post office boxes. He spent a couple of years in a state penitentiary for the drugstore and a few more in federal prison for the post office. A letter from the president came while Don served time in federal prison informing him his country needed him to fight in Southeast Asia. The guards made it clear he wouldn't be able to make the trip, and he better not start any fights in the joint.

During his first stint behind bars, Don made all the promises to himself and his mother every first-time offender makes. He pledged to make something of his life and to never get in trouble with the law again. And he meant it. Every word. And he meant it again when he was back in court less than a year after his release on a new round of charges. Don couldn't stay out of trouble, but he never let it get to him. Each trip back to prison was a little easier than the one before. Every sentence a jury handed down seemed doable, just one of the hazards of the career choice he made.

That was until a judge slammed the gavel down and announced, "Five hundred years." In that moment, Don knew he would never get out of jail. The Oklahoma County district attorney had made sure of that. The DA worked hard to earn his reputation as a man who was tough on crime, and Don became just one more example of this. By the time Don's last case came up before the DA, he was a multiple-time loser who had never held a real job. Sentences of life without the possibility of parole didn't yet exist, but they didn't need to in Oklahoma County. Five hundred years achieved the same purpose. Even with time off for good behavior, Don wouldn't be released until some time after the birth of James T. Kirk, captain of the starship Enterprise. "That woke me up," Don told me in one of the rare occasions he actually talked about his first life. "Of course by then it was too late. I knew I would never again be a free man."

"So what did you do?" I asked.

Don smiled. "Escaped."

Don never told me what he did to get five hundred years, but he did tell me about the escape. He and three friends with long sentences planned it for months. The state pen in MacAlester—known as "Big Mac"—looks like something from a Clint Eastwood movie. Tall, thick brick walls topped with razor wire surround it, with guard towers rising above every corner. Just seeing it from the outside was bad enough. I couldn't imagine becoming a resident. Looking at the walls and the wire, I wondered how anyone could even think about trying to escape. "When all you have to do all day every day for the next five hundred years is stare at that wall," Don said, "you figure a way out. It's not like you have anything else to do."

The prison itself gave Don and his friends their opportunity when they assigned him a job driving a forklift. One night after dark but before final lockdown, Don snuck over to his forklift. He drove it with his friends on it over to a wall, raised it to full extension, and used it as a ladder to go over the wall. "What about the razor wire?" I asked. Don just shrugged. Razor wire isn't much of a barrier to desperate men. "The other three guys went up and over first. Since I was the driver I went last," Don said. "Going up wasn't a problem; coming down was. When I hit the ground I heard a loud crack. I'd shattered one of my legs."

In spite of the pain, he hobbled off into the night. No one stuck around to help him. They may have been friends on the inside, but once over the wall it was every man for himself. Don didn't get far. He found an unlocked pickup truck less than a mile from the prison and climbed inside. Between the cold of the night and the intense throbbing in his leg, he didn't get much sleep his first night as a free man. He finally did doze off just before dawn only to be awakened by the sound of barking dogs and slamming car doors. Don slowly raised up and peeked out the back window. Squad cars surrounded him. "I'd never seen so many guns in my life," Don told me. "Before I even opened the door, I started yelling, 'Don't shoot me, don't shoot me, I give up.'" He stumbled out of the truck, arms lifted high, and fell to the ground as officers piled on top of him.

After spending some time in the prison hospital, Don's trip over the wall earned him a trip to the hole, which was more intense than solitary confinement. A few years after Don's stay there, a judge ordered the state to get rid of it as part of an effort to clean up the prison. The way Don described it, I imagined it was somewhere in the lower bowels of the prison, a dark, damp place even the guards didn't want to enter. The men stayed locked down 24/7. "I was more like an animal than a man by that point," Don told me. "In the hole we'd yell and throw feces at the officers who came down there. And they'd spray us down with fire hoses. It was at that point I pretty much gave up," he said.

Don didn't know it, but at the same time he was going over the wall, his brother was on a plane to California. Seated next to his brother was a pastor from a small Baptist church in Arkansas. During the flight, Don's brother told the pastor the story of his brother who had thrown his life away. The pastor promised to write Don, and he kept his word. With time he even came to Big Mac to see Don. Through the letters and visits, Don eventually decided to turn from his sin and give his life to Jesus Christ. His second life began. "I didn't start running around yelling about Jesus," Don said. "Guys who do don't last long. We all know that sort of thing's pretty much just an act, a way of trying to knock some time off their sentence. No one takes them seriously. And you're just asking for a lot of trouble I didn't want."

Instead, Don went about living the reality of his new life. He stopped acting like an animal locked away for seven lifetimes and began living the life Paul describes in the third chapter of Colossians:

> Since you have been raised to new life with Christ, set your sights on the realities of heaven, where Christ sits at God's right hand in the place of honor and power. Let heaven fill your thoughts. Do not think only about things down here on earth. For you died when Christ died, and your real life is hidden with Christ in God. And when Christ, who is your real life, is revealed to the whole world, you will share in all his glory. (Colossians 3:1-4)

Don Holt took these words to heart. Heaven filled his thoughts, not guard towers and razor wire. He started acting like someone who had died, gone to heaven, and returned to earth. Living in prison became irrelevant to him. When your real life is hidden with Christ in God, it doesn't matter that your address happens to be on cell block A. "I never even thought of asking God to get me out of there," Don confided. "Look, I didn't turn to Christ because I thought God would give me something more than he already gave me. And he'd already given me a lot. I didn't have to get out from behind those walls to be free." He smiled every time he told the story. "I didn't have to get out of prison, because I was already free on the inside."

"Free on the inside" became Don's message to anyone who asked him what was going on in his life. And they asked. Prisoners asked. Guards asked. His family asked. They asked because they started seeing small, subtle changes, like the day Don quit smoking. "I figured that move was pretty basic if I was serious about following Christ." He started attending chapel services and his vocabulary changed. But all of these were minor compared to the most radical difference in Don Holt. Don's entire demeanor was transformed. He truly was a happy man, not happy in the sense of carefree, but happy with a sense of joy and peace most people search for their entire lives. Inside the walls of Big Mac, locked up with the equivalent of seven or eight life sentences, Don found life, real life, the kind of life people run off to the mountains of Tibet hoping they'll find. You could see it in his eyes, and you could hear it in his voice. Although he didn't shout his faith from the top of the wall, he couldn't keep it a secret. He lived a double life, with his real life bubbling over into the life he lived behind the razor wire.

I've never met anyone who really lived as if his life was hidden with Christ in God quite like Don. The state of Oklahoma noticed the change as well. After a few years, they transferred Don to a medium-security prison an hour south of Oklahoma City. It was the same prison the two of us went into together a little more than a year after his release. And he was eventually released. Don's court-ordered attorney won him a hearing before the pardon and parole board. He convinced them Don was a changed man. They agreed, albeit not quite wholeheartedly. They released him on a forty-year parole. "It's doable," Don said, smiling.

Don kept going back to prison even after his release. He couldn't stay away from the joint, although he enjoyed being able to get in his car and drive to his house at the end of the day. We would walk onto the prison yard and heads would snap. Those who'd spent any time at all inside knew Don, and those who hadn't met him knew his story. They flocked to him to see the man who beat a five-hundred-year sentence. All of them wanted to know his secret, and he told them about his double life and the peace he found in Jesus. A few years after Don's release from prison, he went to Wheaton College to prepare for full-time prison ministry. Shortly after graduating, the governor of Oklahoma gave him a full pardon, allowing him to vote for the first time in the 1996 elections.

Don's story doesn't have a Hollywood ending. Around this time, doctors told Don he had cancer, which took his life before his ministry could completely get off the ground. He lived out these words of Christ: "Here on earth you will have many trials and sorrows. But take heart, because I have overcome the world" (John 16:33). God could have worked a miracle and kept the years of abuse Don had heaped on his body from taking their natural toll. But livers give out when bombarded with drugs and alcohol for a long period of time. That's just part of life, just as germs jump off grocery cart handles and give us colds or checks bounce when we have less income than expenses. All are part and parcel of life that always ends. That's reality. But when we belong to Christ, another reality takes over. We possess eternal life. Our lives here on earth aren't just changed; they're exchanged for something far superior.

That's the filter by which we must view everything that happens to us. In Christ we all live a double life. One life we live in the flesh; the other is hidden with Christ in God. Far too often our eyes become fixed on this world, so much so that we wonder where God is and why he's forgotten about us when things take a turn for the worse. Rather than judging everything from the perspective of temporary existence, we need to keep our eyes fixed on our ultimate reality. As Paul wrote to the Colossians, "You died when Christ died, and your real life is hidden with Christ in God" (3:3). Life in the flesh may feel permanent, but it isn't. Keeping our perspective firmly rooted in our real lives in Christ opens the door to accept anything, good or bad, God sends our way.

But that doesn't mean it will be easy. If all the rewards of following Christ—everything that makes saying no to my desires worth it—will not be revealed until heaven, can I handle that? Will I keep following if I don't see any benefits to following Christ now? If God never gives me a taste of heaven, will I keep after him? That's the tension. Yes, I'm supposed to live as if I died, saw heaven, and came back. But I haven't seen heaven, not with my physical eyes. Can faith keep me going without any encouragement along the way?

It did for Don Holt. Whether living in prison with no hope of release or awaiting a liver transplant that never came, he believed that God was in control. I never heard him ask, "Why?" or "Why me?" I can't remember hearing him complain about much of anything. He lived a double life, and he entrusted both lives completely to God. He figured God was on his throne. God knows what he is doing.

PART TWO

CAN I EVER TRUST GOD AGAIN?

Ought not all trials be borne for the sake of everlasting life?

— THOMAS À KEMPIS

CHAPTER 7

GETTING HONEST
WITH GOD

Bad things happen to everyone. That's the reality of living in a fallen world. But for those who belong to Jesus, another reality takes precedence. In this world we will have trouble like everyone else, but take heart: Our Savior overcame the world. The day Jesus walked out of the grave he defeated this evil world. In the process he snatched our lives and hid them in God. We're more than safe. First John 5:4 assures us, "Every child of God defeats this evil world by trusting Christ to give the victory." I love the certainty of the verse. Every child of God defeats this evil world. Every single person born of God wins. It doesn't matter whether we're spiritual giants or only scraping to get by. We all win in Christ. No recounts. No best two out of three. Knowing this gives us the confidence to trust in Christ no matter what the world may throw at us. Paul said it best in the eighth chapter of Romans: "Can anything separate us from Christ's love? Does it mean he no longer loves us if we have trouble or calamity, or are persecuted, or are hungry or cold or in danger or threatened with death? (Even the Scriptures say, 'For your sake we are killed every day; we are being slaughtered like sheep.') No, despite all these things, overwhelming victory is ours through Christ, who loved us" (verses 35-37).

Overwhelming victory is ours! Wow. Not may be ours or could be ours. Overwhelming victory belongs to us right now when we belong to Christ. I'm not some loser struggling to make sense of an out-of-control world. I can hold my head up high, trust in God, and watch him fight my battles. Overwhelming victory is already mine. I like those odds.

Can I be honest? I know the above-mentioned promises are true. If they weren't, how could any of us ever crawl out from under the safety of the covers? But I have trouble taking them to their logical conclusion. Here's my struggle. When hard times hit, I can trust God. I can believe he is on his throne without faltering. In my heart I know beyond a shadow of a doubt that he can take care of me no matter what. But that's only half the battle. Job didn't say, "Shall we trust God in the good times but not in the bad?" I wish he had. No, he asked his wife, "Shall we *accept* good things from God and never anything bad?" I may cling to the hope that God can deliver me, especially when I have nowhere else to turn, but will I accept these trials, these heartaches, these circumstances that I want to go away, will I accept them as the place in life that God has put me today?

That's where all this "overwhelming victory" talk becomes more than words. When life takes a turn for the worse, when a little trouble or calamity or hunger or cold or danger comes my way, I too often do not stand confidently in the overwhelming victory Jesus gives. More times than I want to admit I duck and run for cover. Knowing God's promises should make me some kind of faith superman. But I doubt. I give in to the flood of emotions washing over me. Hard times hit and I fall to the ground and scream at God, asking him what in the world he is doing and why he has to do it to me. *Accept?* Forget it. I just want out.

That's not the worst of it. Even though I panic when trouble strikes me, I'm quick to give advice to others when they hurt. "Just trust God and everything will be all right," I tell them. So do you. We see someone in trouble and think we must give some wise words of spiritual advice. "You know, Jesus already won the war," we'll say. Then we'll smile and give a hug and say, "Everything will be okay." We sound so convincing when our lives are safe and complete. But when we trade places and we're on the receiving end of spiritual clichés, they sound like so much noise. I know I don't want to hear for the thousandth time how God will work everything out when I hurt. For once I would like to be honest enough to tell people to save their breath, to go reassure someone else for a while. Of course, I don't. Few among us say what we all feel when we suffer. Maybe we don't say anything because we don't want to sound like a doubter. I don't want to sound like someone who has never read or doesn't believe the eighth chapter of Romans. What kind of Christian would I be then? Besides, I don't want to hear a voice call down from heaven telling me to stop my whining.

That's why I find myself drawn to Job. He's real. He is honest with both himself and God. Yet his honesty also makes the book that bears his name uncomfortable to read. He doesn't sound like a great person of faith. I love the raw emotion of his speeches — that is, until I finish one and find myself asking, *How can he doubt God? Doesn't Job know what I know? Can't he figure out that his trials came as a means by which God will shut Satan up and put him in his place? How can the greatest believer in all the East, a man at whom God personally pointed and said, "There's no one like him," how can he mutter this?*

> Cursed be the day of my birth, and cursed be the night when
> I was conceived. Let that day be turned to darkness. Let
> it be lost even to God on high, and let it be shrouded in

darkness. Yes, let the darkness and utter gloom claim it for its own. Let a black cloud overshadow it, and let darkness terrify it. Let that night be blotted off the calendar, never again to be counted among the days of the year, never again to appear among the months. . . . Curse it for its failure to shut my mother's womb, for letting me be born to all this trouble. (Job 3:3-6,10)

Cursed be the day of my birth? I wish I'd never been born rather than face this life of trouble? No wonder the three men sitting next to Job on the pile of ashes jumped down his throat. How can the one who asked his wife, "Should we accept only good things from God and never anything bad?" now say, "Why didn't I die at birth as I came from the womb? Why did my mother let me live?" (Job 3:11). The two statements sound incompatible. Eliphaz asked Job what I would like to know: "In the past you have encouraged many a troubled soul to trust in God. . . . But now when trouble strikes, you faint and are broken. Does your reverence for God give you no confidence?" (Job 4:3,5-6). Job sounds weak. Broken. Faithless. Is this what it means to accept bad things from God?

In part, yes. We hear Job's words to his wife and automatically think acceptance means welcoming suffering with open arms. It doesn't. Job pleaded with God to tell him why he was now God's enemy. More than once he expressed his desire to die and get his suffering over with. But one thing he never did: Job never stopped believing. Not once did he shake a fist toward heaven and declare, "There's nobody there; everything I ever believed was a lie." In spite of his pain, in spite of his total exasperation with God, he never turned loose of the Almighty's hand. "Let me argue my case before God," he cried out. "Why are you doing this?" he screamed. Yet he could not turn away from God. He did accept bad things from God, not with a phony smile on his face or with overused clichés falling from his lips. Honestly, painfully, he held on to the Lord.

Job reassures me that I don't have to be strong and unwavering. When my emotions overwhelm me, when the pain becomes more than I can bear, I don't have to bite my lip and call it a blessing. I can pound the floor in the quiet of my room and cry out to God in anger. Lightning didn't blast Job. It won't hit you or me either. After all, God already knows the thoughts racing through our minds. Our questions reach his throne the moment we try to suppress them from ourselves. Job cursed the day of his birth because of his agony, yet God still prevailed in his contest with Satan. You and I can also be real before God. We can express the full force of our pain to him.

What other choice do we have? The idea that we must be brave little troupers only works in fairy tales and B movies. We may be able to keep it up for a while when life takes a turn for the worse. But let the pain become sharp enough, difficult enough, and we'll cry out. The words may not exactly qualify as a prayer. They go deeper than "And God, please help me through this difficult time I'm going through." The greater the pain, the more primal the words, if we can utter anything at all. I'm speaking for myself. You may be that exceptional person of faith who finds joy and happiness in your darkest hours. Call me weak, but I can't act like that. I cannot pretend before God or hold my tongue. What I feel spills out before him.

And in moments of suffering I feel doubt. I start to wonder about God as strange thoughts race through my mind. *How can God say he loves me and throw me into this? Where is the power of God I've heard about all my life? If God is so mighty, why doesn't he do something?* While I've never doubted his existence or the gift of his Son, I have wondered about his character. There have been times, more than I want to admit to myself, when I've looked around at where he's taken me and wondered if he is trustworthy, if I wouldn't have been better off ignoring his plans. Heaven and salvation I want. I can live without the pain caused by living according to his plan.

I also feel sad. Suffering brings a sadness words cannot describe. "Consider it all joy, my brothers, when you encounter trials of various kinds," James wrote (1:2). Considering something to be joy doesn't mean feeling anything approaching joy. Suffering brings a deep, crushing sorrow. Words can't express it. Who would understand? The pain of suffering pulls us inward. We don't think anyone could ever relate to what we feel, especially other Christians. What kind of believer can I possibly be if I'm battling depression—depression brought on by the trials I'm supposed to count as joy?

All this makes me feel very alone. Suffering is a solitary business. No matter how many people gather around to console us, we feel like a huge wall stands between them and us. In the middle of writing this book, I found myself in a living room with a couple whose fourteen-year-old daughter died in a car wreck the day before. I went to their home to comfort a grieving father and mother, to try to share in their pain and give them hope. After all, I had a fourteen-year-old daughter. My daughter's high school locker was next to their daughter's. If anyone should be able to relate, I thought, it would be me. One look into the father's eyes and I knew I couldn't even guess as to the depth of his pain. Friends went in and out of the house, and although they felt a great deal of grief over the girl's death, they were still able to go home at the end of the day and get on with their lives. The father and mother I left in the house would never again experience a truly normal day. Their pain separated them from everyone else around them. It even built a wall between the two of them. You see this same isolation in Job. Three friends gather around him, but they can't relate, they can't understand, they don't know what he is going through. Job faces his darkest hour alone.

Pain also creates anger. You hear it rise up in Job's speeches. He doesn't cry like a spoiled child pulled from his favorite toy. In Job we hear the sad disappointment of a betrayed lover. I've been mad at God although I tried to pretend I wasn't. Not long after I originally wrote this chapter, the editor of *Discipleship Journal* asked me to write an article about how to overcome feelings of anger toward God. She'd read one of the early drafts of the book, so she thought she knew what to expect. A few weeks after I e-mailed her my article, she called. "Uhhh, Mark," she stammered around the reason she'd called. Finally she blurted it out. "This article of yours isn't going to work because you are just *too* angry." And here's the kicker: I had no idea that's how I really felt until I put the words down on paper. I had just come out of a four-year-long trial that I thought would never end. Until that moment, I did not realize I was angry at God. Very angry. Once I finally worked through the anger and disappointment I felt toward God, I had to come back and change this part of the chapter. I originally planned to scoot right through here and pretend this is a problem other people have. I tried to pretend that I did not feel the emotions boiling inside of me. I tried to convince myself that my anger didn't exist. I pushed it down and kept up the good Christian front. And I avoided God. I prayed, but I avoided the heart-to-heart, honest conversations with him because I was afraid of what I might say. I wanted to tell him, "You're unfair. You're cruel. How can you call yourself a loving God and do this?" No one says such things to God. But Job did. He said what I've thought but couldn't bring myself to say for the longest time. Funny, it wasn't until I got honest with God that our relationship was repaired and the anger went away.

I apologize for getting sidetracked. I didn't mean to dwell on anger, because it is only one of the emotions that come washing over us when life hurts. Doubt, sorrow, isolation, anger—you and I feel all of these and a thousand other emotions when bad things from the hand of God overtake us. We become angry with God for throwing us into this mess and angry at ourselves for not handling it better. That's the kind of raw emotion we hear in Job.

Job may be more intense than other characters in the Bible, but he isn't alone in speaking up. Paul complained to God. In his second letter to the church in Corinth, Paul describes his daily battle with an unnamed trial he calls "a messenger of Satan." Whatever it was, Paul's daily battle with it drove him to his knees pleading with God to take it away. God never did. Three times Paul begged for relief, and three times God responded, "My gracious favor is all you need. My power works best in your weakness" (12:9). If Paul had been the brave little trouper we think we need to be when bad things come our way, he never would have asked — even once. Instead he would have smiled and told everyone what a blessing his weakness was. It seems to have taken a long time for him to accept his thorn in the flesh as a gift from God. First he pleaded and begged and cried out to God, "Take this thing away!" Then he begged and pleaded and cried some more. Finally, after he knew God wouldn't change his answer, Paul declared, "Now I am glad to boast about my weaknesses, so that the power of Christ may work through me. Since I know it is all for Christ's good, I am quite content with my weaknesses and with insults, hardships, persecutions, and calamities. For when I am weak, then I am strong" (verses 9-10). If we didn't know about his personal struggle, we wouldn't be able to relate to Paul's words. Knowing his struggle not only with pain but also with God makes his words even more powerful.

We hear the same anguish in Jesus the night before his crucifixion. "My soul is crushed to the point of grief," he told his disciples (Matthew 26:38). He fell on his face in the Garden of Gethsemane and pleaded with his Father, "Abba, Father, everything is possible for you. Please take this cup of suffering from me" (Mark 14:36). Jesus' pain grew so intense that sweat poured off his forehead like drops of blood. The writer of the book of Hebrews tells us that Jesus endured the cross and despised its shame "because of the joy he knew would be his afterward" (12:2). Jesus doesn't look joyful in the garden or on the cross crying out, "My God, my God, why have you forsaken me!" (Matthew 27:46). Yet no matter how intense his pain became, he would not allow it to keep him from doing his Father's will. He accepted his suffering as from God.

This same tension builds within us as we try to act on God's promises and accept whatever he sends our way. We know that our real lives are hidden with Christ in God. Deep down we long to have the reality of eternal life define who we are and how we respond to suffering. Count it all joy, James tells us. Rejoice in trials, Paul reminds us in the books of Romans and Philippians. We want to. We want to be brave. We want to be strong. And we become frustrated because we are all too human.

We don't have to put on a front. When the pain becomes more than we can bear, we can let it out to God without worrying that he will reject us for being real. Crying out, asking God why, pounding the floor in anger and frustration—none of these shows a lack of faith. Nor will God reject us as a result. In fact, the opposite is the case. Paul found in his moment of greatest weakness that God's strength more than made up the difference. The ability to believe and cling to the promises of God depends not on our strength but on the strength of God. He doesn't reject us when we question his fairness or justice.

Look at the end of the book of Job. After the dust clears, God commends Job once again. Why? Because Job, like Jesus and Paul, accepted the turn of events in his life as God's will. Not with some phony, plastic smile pasted on his face but with his real, gut-level honest emotions pouring out toward God.

After all the complaints, all the tears, all the questions of why and wondering if I've messed up, I choose to accept this place of sorrow and pain as the place God wants me. The Bible portrays the Christian walk as a journey, with God leading the way. If I trust him enough to believe he knows what he is doing and where we are going, I must accept the difficult roads as readily as I accept gentle downhill glides. Even though I'm in pain, God led me here. He must want me here.

It isn't easy. What an understatement. I don't feel brave and I do a poor imitation of an overwhelming victor. God never tells me I have to be one. He leads the way. I follow him. When he takes me through the darkest valley, I close my eyes, cling to his hand, and recite his promises. He knows where we need to go. Rather than complain or put on some phony front, I choose to trust his wisdom and accept this part of the trip. I won't run away. I will try to see this place through God's eyes even as my tears cloud my vision.

CHAPTER 8

MUST GOD SEEM GOOD
FOR ME TO BELIEVE?

All this talk about doubt and sorrow and loneliness and anger makes me nervous. I need some reassurance here. Tell me I don't need to be nervous about following God because he is good. Right? That's why I can trust him. He's good and loving and merciful and gracious. Everything I think I know about God screams that he cannot be anything but. You might as well ask if the sky has to be blue or the ocean salty if you have to ask if God must be good. He cannot be anything but, anymore than the sky can turn neon green on a clear day or the oceans can fill themselves with fresh water. God is good. Even that is an understatement. God is good. I feel a little silly even bringing it up.

Could you imagine a god who wasn't good? He would foil Einstein and play dice with the universe. Every day would bring a new set of terrors as an evil god toyed with his creation. One day up would be up, the next day down. Everything would be in flux. The pitiful creatures who lived in such a world would long for death, thinking it better than life. Of course they would be wrong. Imagine falling into the hands of an evil god. What kinds of cruel torture would he inflict throughout all of eternity on frail creatures of dust? The torment probably wouldn't last forever, though. A bad god, a mean god, would probably grow bored with the whole experiment of humanity and destroy everything before moving on to his next sadistic project.

None of this describes the God of the Bible. He is merciful, kind, and gracious. Above all, he is good. This is still a serious understatement. I need to find something stronger, something like this: God is love. He doesn't just love or feel love or express love; he *is* love. Love defines his character. Everything he does will always be an expression of his love. And he loves me.

"God is love" is not some far-off concept. He draws near to us, to you and me, and loves us personally. He loves us with the tender care of a father, the passion of a bridegroom, and the compassion of a friend. The love he has for us expresses itself daily through sacrifice. He gives and gives and gives. The greatest gift he ever gave was his Son who died in our place. Why? Because "he loved us and sent his Son," as 1 John 4:10 tells us. My daughters learned this verse at the age of four. It was one of the first Bible verses they ever memorized. What better place to start?

I know God is love because he loved me before I loved him. Love always starts with God, not us. If we had to take the first step, no one would ever come close to anything that could be described as love for God. John said it best in 1 John 4:19: "First we were loved, now we love. He loved us first" (MSG). If God were a human being, we would call him shameless. After all, he chases us down, relentlessly pursuing us to make us his own. We don't realize he's chasing us until after we're caught. Once we're in his arms, we don't complain. Sometimes we think we're the ones who pursue God, but we aren't. He pulls us in with a glimpse of his greatness. The first taste of his love hooks us. His beauty attracts us, calls us, and fills our hearts with a burning desire that can be satisfied only by God himself.

He loved us first, but as we fall into his arms, we don't feel like pressing the point. It doesn't matter who started the romance; we're just glad to be included. Deep down we know we don't deserve this. God had to chase us because we ran from him and into the arms of another. Although God created you and me to know him and love him, we didn't want anything to do with him. We're like Adam and Eve back in the garden, trying to replace God with ourselves. We rebel. God loves us anyway. He loves us right back into his arms.

And that's why we love him and trust him and follow him. We do so because God is good. He showered his love upon us; we finally reciprocated. His goodness and mercy and grace precede our belief just as surely as planting precedes harvest. If he hadn't made the first move, we would still be wandering around lost. We can't take any pride in this. I feel more than a little foolish thinking I ran from God. But I did. You did too. Psalm 53:2-3 breaks the news to us this way: "God looks down from heaven on the entire human race; he looks to see if there is even one with real understanding, one who seeks for God. But no, all have turned away from God; all have become corrupt." The good news is that God chased us down. Now that we're caught, we enjoy all the fruits of being loved unconditionally by the Lord of the universe. He took the initiative; we reap the benefits.

God is good. I know it because God loves me — not in theory but in fact. He chased me down when I ran from him. He loved me when I wanted him to leave me alone. His love so overpowers me that I must love him back. I know God is good because I've felt it, I've tasted it, I've experienced it firsthand. Don't confuse me with talk of bad things coming from the hand of God. The only reason I believe is because God loves me. I know it sounds bad, but I don't feel any shame admitting it. God is good and I believe in him.

But does God have to continually do good things for me to keep me? If he started acting in a way that appeared to me to be less than good, would I continue to follow him? The question isn't whether God is good. The real issue, the question Satan raised in the first chapter of Job, is this: Has God bribed us into loving him? Listen to Satan's accusation against Job: "Yes, Job fears God," Satan said to the Lord, "but not without good reason. You've always protected him and his home and his property from harm. You have made him prosperous in everything he does. Look how rich he is!" (Job 1:9-10). Satan accused God of buying Job's devotion and, by implication, ours as well. Essentially, he said, "The only reason anyone sticks with you is because you bribe them."

That's the real question we can't get away from. Yes, we love God because he first loved us. We didn't pursue him; he pursued us. Our salvation, our relationship with God, all came about because God initiated it. But why do we stick with him? Does God have to continue to shower you and me with gifts to hold our affection? We know no one would come to Christ if not for the powerful, active love of the Father. Sin so blinds our eyes that we choose death over life until he lifts the veil. Yet once our eyes are open, what keeps us in God's camp?

A cat showed up on my doorstep when I was about ten years old. I don't know where he came from. He just appeared out of the blue. Like any self-respecting ten-year-old, I immediately set out a saucer of milk. The cat knew he had found a new home. My sisters and I named him Fluffy, after a lion in a Tony Randall movie, because he resembled a lion with yellow fur and a long crop of hair around his neck like a mane. Although officially listed as an outside pet, Fluffy spent most of his time in the house with us. He made himself right at home with the rest of the pets in our house. One afternoon he jumped on top of the goldfish bowl and splashed out most of the water trying to catch my sister's goldfish. Another day he destroyed my hamster's cage and chased him around my room. Luckily Hamlet the hamster got away; otherwise this story would have a much different ending.

Everyone in the family loved Fluffy. We fed him and babied him and allowed him to establish himself as king of the household, much to my dog's chagrin. Then about a year after he showed up, he wandered away, never to be seen again. He probably found himself a new home with another ten-year-old who happened to set out a bowl of milk. Stray cats are like that. They go wherever their stomachs take them. If only my mother hadn't bought cheap cat food, Fluffy might have stuck around long enough to catch the goldfish and hamster. But she had, and he set off in search of a better offer.

The book of Job forces me to ask myself, *Am I a spiritual Fluffy? Does believing have to be beneficial for me to keep after it?* Before you immediately say no, take a few moments to let the question sink in. I'm not asking if you have to become as rich as Job to stay with God, although the average American is very wealthy in comparison to the rest of the world. Most of us don't expect gold and silver to rain down from heaven on us, but we do want to see some tangible benefits for following Christ. We want something to assure us we aren't wasting our time. It doesn't have to be much. An answer to prayer. A sense of purpose. A happy ending to a difficult trial. Something. Anything.

But what if we never saw any tangible benefits to following Christ? Would we keep on? Would we accept his plan when it made life more difficult from a purely human perspective? That's the heart of Satan's accusations against Job. Even after all of Job's wealth was stripped away, after his ten children and all of his servants and shepherds lay dead, Satan accused God of buying Job's love. Job had nothing left but his health, and the accuser wanted to take it away too. "Skin for skin — he blesses you only because you bless him," Satan replied to the Lord. "A man will give up everything he has to save his life. But take away his health, and he will surely curse you to your face" (Job 2:4-5). Job's children were dead. His flocks and camels and herds disappeared in a combination of thievery and natural disasters. He had nothing but his health, and Satan viewed that as a celestial bribe through which God bought Job's devotion.

> "All right, do with him as you please," the Lord said to Satan. "But spare his life." So Satan left the LORD's presence, and he struck Job with a terrible case of boils from head to foot. (Job 2:6-7)

I've never considered the absence of boils to be one of the big benefits of following Christ. After forty years of attending church, I can't remember ever hearing someone stand up to give a testimony saying, "I lost my job, my house, my family, my car. Everything I own is gone. But, boy oh boy, God sure has been good to me because I'm not covered with scabs." You may have everything when you have your health, but if you have nothing else, most of us would call that a bad day. How long will we stick with the Lord under such conditions?

The drama played out in the life of Job, but the question continues to hang over everyone who follows Christ by faith. Do we believe because of the blessings God gives? Do we follow his Son because he will give us a better life? Yes, God is good, and we readily accept all the good things he gives us like a child tearing open presents on Christmas morning. But does he have to be good to me for me to stick with him? Is it Jesus we love, or do we love the joy and the peace and the forgiveness and the freedom he gives? Does God have to be good to me in order for me to accept his will for my life, or will I continue to trust him even if doing so does me no good at all?

My freshman English teacher talked a lot about her faith in Christ. Asking her questions about God beat discussing *A Tale of Two Cities*, so we pressed her about why she believed. Halfway through the second semester, she finally ended all the discussions with the statement, "Even if Christianity were proved to be false, it gives you such a good life that I would still believe it." Her answer took me back even as a know-it-all fourteen-year-old. More than thirty years later I can still hear her words ringing in my ears. I don't remember much else from the class, but I'll never forget her answer. She wanted to convey the depth of her devotion to Christ, to show she would stick with him even if someone found his body in a tomb. "I don't need facts to believe," she tried to say, but something else entirely came across.

In effect, my freshman English teacher displayed something far below devotion. Yes, Christianity is beneficial and God is good. But finding something helpful is not the same as finding it to be true. We first come to Christ because the love of God pulls us in. He becomes our passion, our greatest and only desire. Becoming a believer isn't like joining the Daughters of the American Revolution or the Optimist Club. It is a love story in which we play the part of the unlovable maiden made beautiful by the love of the perfect Lover. Yet this relationship is more than a matter of the emotions or the heart. It boils down to a question of truth. Christianity purports to explain the deepest mysteries of the universe, from the dawn of creation through the end of all physical matter. The story of Jesus claims to be the ultimate truth. God became flesh and dwelt among us. The God-man died on a cross for the sins of the world. Three days later he rose from the dead. One day he will return to judge every person who has ever drawn a breath. These statements are either facts or lies. They cannot be both. There are benefits in believing, but that does not make the statements true.

My freshman English teacher essentially said that Christianity didn't have to be true for her to believe; it just has to be helpful. This misses the mark entirely. C. S. Lewis said it best in his essay "Man or Rabbit":

Christianity claims to give an account of facts — to tell you what the real universe is like. Its account of the universe may be true, or it may not, and once the question is really before you, then your natural inquisitiveness must make you want to know the answer. If Christianity is untrue, then no honest man will want to believe it, however helpful it might be; if it is true, every honest man will want to believe it, even if it gives him no help at all.[1]

Job stands out as one of the greatest heroes of the faith because his devotion could not be bought. When he lost everything, he continued to praise the Lord. Don't think he sat back with a smile on his face, waved his arm in the air, and said (and you really need to supply a thick Bible-thumper accent when you say these words), "Praise God, everything's gonna be fine. Hal-le-lu-YAH, God is good!" Come on, let's be realistic. Job ached in the deepest recesses of his soul. The pain that kept him up all night and wore him out through the day had more to do with the anguish of his heart than the boils on his body. He suffered under more than grief. Suddenly Job found himself cut off from God himself.

God ceased being good to Job, yet Job did not abandon him. His inability to stop believing created a greater set of problems. "Curse God and die," his wife said (Job 2:9). Get it over with. God hates you; that's apparent. Hate him back. Tell him to leave you alone once and for all, and lie down and die. But Job couldn't. Everything around him screamed that all he ever believed about God was a lie. His integrity, his sacrifices, his devotion, all lay in the dust, worthless. Yet he never cursed God to his face, as Satan predicted. He continued to believe even though his faith and devotion increased the anguish of his soul. Job found he had no other choice. Faith in God no longer provided any tangible benefits, but that didn't change the fact it was still true.

I know God is good, but must God always be good to me before I will accept the twists and turns of life he leads me through? If so, I am in trouble because God cannot and will not always do that which appears from my limited human perspective to be loving and kind. At times his actions will seem harsh and painful. They must if God is to act in ways that are truly good. George MacDonald describes this paradox in *At the Back of the North Wind*. The book tells the story of a boy named Diamond, who develops a relationship with the North Wind, who represents God. The boy wants to go away with the beautiful North Wind because of the goodness she's showered upon him. Diamond tells her:

> "Well, I will go with you because you are beautiful and good, too."
>
> "Ah, but there's another thing, Diamond: What if I should look ugly without being bad — look ugly myself because I am making ugly things beautiful? — What then?"
>
> "I don't quite understand you, North Wind. You tell me what then."
>
> "Well, I will tell you. If you see me with my face all black, don't be frightened. If you see me flapping wings like a bat's, as big as the whole sky, don't be frightened. If you hear me raging ten times worse than Mrs. Bill, the blacksmith's wife — even if you see me looking in at people's windows like Mrs. Eve Dropper, the gardener's wife — you must believe that I am doing my work. Nay, Diamond, if I change into a serpent or a tiger, you must not let go your hold of me, for my hand will never change in yours if you keep a good hold. If you keep a hold,

you will know who I am all the time, even when
you look at me and can't see me the least like the
North Wind. I may look something very awful. Do
you understand?"[2]

I can think of no better picture to describe what it means to
accept both good and bad from the hand of God. Doing so is not
surrendering to fate or giving up on all prospects for ever tasting joy
or happiness in this life. No, it is keeping hold of God even when he
sometimes does not appear to be the good God of love. We can accept
bad things from the hand of God as we accept the fact that God has
not changed. As we cling to him, we cling to the hope that he is who
he is all the time, even when we can't see even the least of the God
we know is there.

Must God be good for me to believe? The answer will be revealed
only when my life takes an unexpected turn and God appears to be
less than good from my limited, human perspective.

CHAPTER 9

THE PROMISE THAT NEVER FAILS (NO MATTER HOW DARK THE DAY MAY BE)

Every day Sally told Maurice she loved him, but he never reciprocated. Most days he hardly acknowledged her presence, but Sally kept right on. Day after day she went out of her way to see him, and day after day Maurice barely noticed. From time to time Sally would bring him a little gift, never anything big, just something to show him she loved him. The only gift Maurice ever gave Sally was a small smile or the gift of his attention, however brief it might be.

Yet Sally's love never faded. It didn't matter to her that a stroke had taken away most of the man she married more than fifty years earlier. He couldn't speak, and he had lost all use of his left side. A feeding tube kept Maurice alive, along with the round-the-clock care he received in the nursing home. But to Sally, the man she loved was still inside the body trapped in the hospital bed, and she was determined to keep on loving him. She had no other choice. Long before, in a church in southwestern Oklahoma, she made a promise to Maurice as he did to her. Both pledged to love one another and to remain faithful in good times and bad, in prosperity and adversity, in sickness and in health. One world war, three children, and two strokes later, nothing had changed. Sally kept her promise and continued to love her husband even though she wasn't always sure he knew who she was.

Don't think for a moment it was easy for her. Immediately after Maurice's stroke, all their friends regularly visited the two of them in the Sequoia View Hospital ICU. Sally never left Maurice's side. Once or twice she broke down, wondering if he would ever come home, unsure if she had the strength to keep on going. Somehow she found the strength, even after most people stopped dropping by, even after it became clear he would have to remain in a nursing home. Sally did eventually find a way to bring her husband home. Stubborn to a fault, she refused to accept anything as impossible. With her daughter Mary, a heart specialist from Southern California, at her side, she convinced the doctors to let Maurice come home for a birthday celebration. It was his last trip.

From that point forward, Sally had to content herself with visits at the nursing home. Although Maurice lost all ability to communicate, she never acted as though his body was a hollow shell from which her beloved had already departed. Every day she would read him the mail and bring him up to date on everything happening in their small California mountain town. In the spring and fall, she would badger the nurses to place Maurice in a wheelchair so she could take him outside. There, under a eucalyptus tree, she would sit beside him, hold his hand, and read him the newspaper — two old lovers enjoying one another.

Sally didn't spend hours on end at a nursing home because she thought she would absolutely die if she didn't see her Maurice. I never knew her to lose herself scribbling his name over and over and over on her notebook. The thrill of romance didn't drive her; love did. Love this strong doesn't happen by chance. Sally loved Maurice because she chose to. Each and every day, year after year, she chose to love the man to whom she had pledged her life, no matter how much pain and grief the choice caused her. She did it because she promised him she would.

During the last two years of Maurice's life, Sally couldn't do much for him. She couldn't break through the fog the stroke created, nor could she find some miracle drug to bring him back to her. No matter how much she coaxed him, restoring movement to his left side remained impossible. Medically she couldn't do anything. His greatest needs went beyond all her hopes and prayers. All she could really do was be there with him. More than once she told me she couldn't stand the thought of Maurice lying in a hospital bed all alone. "If I don't do anything else," she said with strong resolution in her voice, "I will be there with him, no matter what." Sally kept her promise even up to the moment Maurice slipped out of this life and into the life to come.

I know of no better picture of how God reacts to the suffering we face in this life. Even when it appears he will do nothing else, God stays beside us. Although this may seem like a small thing on the outside of suffering looking in, it is one of the greatest gifts of his grace. And like all of God's gifts, we must never take it for granted. We can't command the Lord of the universe to get over to our house when a phone call shatters our world. He stays beside us because he chooses to, not because he must. Long ago he made us a promise. Jesus' last recorded words in the book of Matthew convey his pledge: "Be sure of this: I am with you always, even to the end of the age" (28:20).

"I am with you always," he promised. "Good times and bad." When we feel we have the world on a string, and on days we feel as if the world has wrapped itself around our throats, he is there. "I will not abandon you as orphans," Jesus vowed (John 14:18). Because of this promise, we will never experience one moment of separation from him. Like this loving wife beside the bed of her dying husband, God shares whatever suffering we may face. Paul called him the source of every mercy and the God who comforts us in all our troubles (see 2 Corinthians 1:3-4). It is a promise he will not break, the promise that makes it possible to accept every step of the journey as God's will for our lives.

It is at this point that many people walk away from God disappointed. We look to him for comfort and we try to hang on to the promise of his presence, but as days turn into weeks and nothing changes, we want something more than his attention. Unlike Sally watching a stroke pull more and more of her husband away from her, God has the power to do something dramatic. He created the world out of nothing in six days; certainly he can fix whatever we face today. Why doesn't he? Even if we must increase our faith to accept our present suffering as God's will for our lives, can't he speed up the journey to the next stage, the less painful part of the journey? After we find him faithful, why can't we experience the joy of watching him perform a miracle? The longer we hurt, the more time that passes with our suffering intensifying each day, we start to wonder why God doesn't act.

We wonder because he has made more than one promise to us. In our dark moments we hear these promises over and over. Well-meaning friends who drop by the hospital waiting room remind us of other guarantees we believe we have from God. "God will work everything out for the best," they say in a loose paraphrase of Romans 8:28. Or they remind us that "God has a purpose in everything that happens to us." If we wait long enough, we'll see it, just as Joseph watched his brothers' treachery become the means by which God saved the world. When we feel like giving up, someone always reminds us, "God won't put more on you than you can bear," a less-than-accurate reference to 1 Corinthians 10:13, which tells us God will not allow us to be tempted beyond that which we can endure. As days turn into weeks and our strength starts to slip, we also hear how "God rewards faithfulness." I heard this a lot from fellow pastors as the church I served weathered a full-fledged spiritual assault.

All God's other promises give us hope for something more than comfort. They tell us God can and will act on our behalf. It doesn't matter who is against us. God is for us. Soon he will arise and stand with us. We don't have to surrender and accept this horrible lot in life as God's final chapter for us. One day soon our enemies will flee as God fights our battles, even if we aren't quite sure who or what our enemies may be. He will work everything out for the best. He will show everyone how he planned all along to work through our tragedy. Our strength won't give out because God won't put more on us than we are able to carry. In the end, he will reward our faithfulness.

Or will he?

Job's three friends were certain God always rewards those who stay faithful to him and always punishes those who reject him. Eliphaz urged Job to admit his fault and turn back to God. Then Job would discover how God . . .

> will rescue you again and again so that no evil can touch you. He will save you from death in time of famine, from the power of the sword in time of war. You will be safe from slander and will have no fear of destruction when it comes. You will laugh at destruction and famine; wild animals will not terrify you. You will be at peace with the stones of the field, and its wild animals will be at peace with you. You will know that your home is kept safe. When you visit your

pastures, nothing will be missing. Your children will be many; your descendants will be as plentiful as grass! You will live to a good old age. You will not be harvested until the proper time! (Job 5:19-26)

Eliphaz's logic has only one flaw: Job was faithful to the Lord. It didn't matter, though. Evil still wiped out everything he had. The sword devastated his home. Destruction took away all his possessions in one day. Job never felt peace; he never felt security. All day every day he was haunted by fear and the jeers of people around him. His home had not been kept safe. Everything was missing from his pastures. And his children, though once many, were all dead. If God always rewards faithfulness, none of these things would have happened.

Job isn't alone. Throughout the Bible we find people who clung to the Lord yet their lives were destroyed. Blessings and joy and prosperity gave way to suffering and heartache and tragedy. Isaiah stood for the Lord when few other prophets would speak out, yet tradition tells us an unhappy mob stuffed him in a hollow tree and sawed him in half. Stephen spoke out boldly for Christ in the midst of the Jewish reigning council. They stoned him to death rather than accept Jesus as the Messiah. James was part of the inner circle of the disciples along with his brother John and Simon Peter. He also bears the distinction of being the first of the apostles to die, put to death by Herod a few years after Jesus rose from the dead. Paul himself died as a martyr in Rome. He wrote to Timothy shortly before his death, "The first time I was brought before the judge, no one was with me. Everyone had abandoned me" (2 Timothy 4:16). If God rewards faithfulness in this life, he has a funny way of showing it.

Others may tell us God won't lay more on us than we are able to carry, but they can't feel the weight crushing our shoulders. Job told Eliphaz, Bildad, and Zophar: "I do not have the strength to endure.

I do not have a goal that encourages me to carry on. Do I have strength as hard as stone? Is my body made of bronze? No, I am utterly helpless, without any chance of success" (Job 6:11-13).

While three men whose homes were intact and whose children played in their backyards looked on, Job felt his knees giving way and his faith crumbling. In that moment, words such as "God won't put more on you than you can bear" rang hollow. Job knew his breaking point, and he had already surpassed it.

Yet the bottom line is this: God's promises go beyond this temporary world of time and firmly plant us in eternity, which we will spend in his presence. Second Corinthians 4:16-18 promises,

> Though our bodies are dying, our spirits are being renewed every day. For our present troubles are quite small and won't last very long. Yet they produce for us an immeasurably great glory that will last forever! So we don't look at the troubles we can see right now; rather, we look forward to what we have not yet seen. For the troubles we see will soon be over, but the joys to come will last forever.

The suffering we endure in this world may seem to last forever, but when God gives the grace to see it from his persepctive, we find that it is short-lived compared to what he has in store for those who love him. Yes, God will cause everything to work together for good for those who love him and are called according to his purpose, just as Romans 8:28 promises. That doesn't mean everything will work out for the best in this life. Far from it. God works on the scale of the world to come. The worst this world can dish out, death, Paul calls far better than life because it ushers us into the presence of Christ (see Philippians 1:21). The good for which God works doesn't guarantee happiness or comfort or miracles today. He works toward a far more permanent good.

The same holds true for his purpose behind all the things that happen to us. He has a master plan, but that doesn't mean we will ever understand it this side of eternity. We can drive ourselves crazy looking for some small clue to help us unlock the mystery of why life has turned out how it has. I know. I used to think helping people solve the puzzle was part of my job as the comforting pastor sitting beside them at all hours of the night in hospital waiting rooms. "God has a purpose. God has a plan," I would boldly say. Yet the more trips I made to hospitals and funeral homes, the less confident I became. I know that God has a purpose in everything that happens—he never plays dice with the universe. I'm just not too sure what it may be. I have no clue how God could work through a forty-nine-year-old's fatal heart attack or what plan God might have for the forty-year-old widow and eleven-year-old daughter who suddenly face life alone. And that's just it. We can't know. God never tells us what he is up to.

Yet one promise bridges the gap between eternity and today. "I am with you always," Jesus said (Matthew 28:20). Through the presence of the Holy Spirit in the life of every believer, we never go through one moment separated from the one who loves us. As Paul reassures us in the eighth chapter of Romans, nothing in heaven or earth can change this. Trouble, calamity, hunger, persecution, even death—nothing can separate us from God's loving presence. This doesn't mean he is as helpless as a grieving wife asking the doctors for some kind of miracle. He could cause blood clots to dissolve and neurological damage to mend. Sometimes he does. We call those miracles. Yet the miraculous actually takes less faith than the protracted agony of watching someone we love suffer, waiting for the inevitable, clinging to God even though we can't feel his presence.

I watched Sally with Maurice. Every day she took her place beside his bed. There were days he barely awoke. If by some miracle he had recovered, he probably never would remember the days and weeks and years she spent at his side. It didn't matter to Sally whether he knew she was there. She always was. Always. She refused to leave his side.

God keeps the same promise to us. We may not feel it. A sharp zing of joy doesn't have to shoot down our spine. Clinging to God through tragedy doesn't always feel like a particularly religious event. As we've already discovered, many days we feel totally alone, completely isolated from God and everyone else. But our feelings do not negate God's promise. He vowed to stay with us and he will, even if everything around us screams that he has abandoned us. I will always be with you, he says. He doesn't have to be. He stays there because he promised he would.

God's presence gives us the grace to accept every step of the journey as his will for our lives. You and I may never know why the path had to be so painful, but by faith we know he is beside us. This promise, above all others, has the power to carry us through whatever life may bring.

CHAPTER 10

WHY DOESN'T GOD DO SOMETHING (IF HE CAN)?

So why doesn't God do something? Why doesn't he prevent trees from falling on cars or protect an eight-year-old boy from dying alone on a hillside after his four-wheeler flips on top of him? Why doesn't God stop rare genetic defects that guarantee a baby will not live more than a few hours? Why? Why doesn't he keep mothers and fathers who both profess to be his followers from fighting all the time and eventually splitting up? Why doesn't he end wars and famines and diseases? Does he not care about the four-year-old girl who is dragged kicking and screaming into a car from which she will not emerge alive? Surely he's noticed the thousands of women being raped in the Congo as an act of war or the millions dying of AIDS in East Africa. If he does, why doesn't he do something? Accept bad things from the hand of God, Job tells us, yet why should we? God is all-powerful and all-knowing; his presence permeates every corner of creation. Why doesn't he just eliminate bad things from the world? If he can, why doesn't he?

All around us, people suffer and die while God seems to do nothing—nothing, that is, except possibly send suffering and death our way. Job believed that God was responsible for all the problems that struck his life. "Leave me alone, God," he cried out. Looking heavenward, Job saw God sitting on a cloud dropping thunderbolts of pain on top of his head. Yet even as he cried for relief, he spoke as though God had some reason for his tragedy. This hope lies beneath his words to his wife, "Should we accept only good things from the hand of God and never anything bad?" Accept them, embrace them, receive bad things as readily as we receive all of God's blessings. Both good things and bad come from the hand of God, Job believed, and we need to treat them as such.

Can we expect people to live this way? Talking about God's higher purposes in suffering is easy. Living through it and taking such ideas to their logical conclusion is much more difficult. Accepting bad things from God implies not only divine sanction but also divine action in both personal tragedies and horrific events in history. To confidently say that God permits difficult days into the lives of people is to say that God had a hand in the Holocaust. On a human level, Hitler's ideology along with his and his minions' satanic cruelty, coupled with simple inaction on the part of ordinary citizens, murdered six million Jews. Yet isn't God also culpable if we believe that bad things come from his hand as readily as good? None of us would say God found pleasure in one of the darkest hours of human history any more than he enjoyed watching Job's family die. However, insisting God has a purpose in everything that happens—that all things, good or bad, ultimately come from his hand either through direct acts or through lending his consent to others—seems to imply that God in some way wanted the Holocaust to occur.

Did he?

If he did, did he also want 9/11 or the Cambodian killing fields or ethnic cleansing in the Balkans? Did God will AIDS into existence and predetermine that it should wipe out huge sections of Africa's population? Did God choose to allow the bubonic and pneumonic plagues to wipe out one-third of the population of Europe along with millions in Asia in the fourteenth century? It happened so long ago that we forget that the Black Death made all the cruelties of the twentieth century seem minor. One-half of the population of Italy died. In some parts of England, the death toll reached 90 percent. Europe ran out of pickmen, those paid to bury the dead, leaving bodies to pile up and rot in the streets. Everyone suffered. Every family experienced death. One man wrote after burying five of his children with his own hands, "No bells tolled and nobody wept no matter what his loss because almost everyone expected death."[1] So many people died from the plague that almost everyone believed it had to be the end of the world. Was God responsible for their pain?

Comparing the suffering of a solitary individual to global epidemics may seem too much of a reach. Or is it? The story of the Black Death or AIDS or 9/11 goes beyond statistics. Ultimately, all are collections of the tales of individuals and families touched by tragedy. They are the combined stories of hundreds and thousands and millions of Jobs. Standing at a distance, we wonder why so many have to suffer; those in the middle of it wonder why their husband or wife or child died. Each one wrestles with his or her own questions of why God would allow this tragedy to sweep them away. The Bible tells us about only Job. I have to wonder how many other families were wiped out by the raiding bands of Chaldeans. Did the storm that caused Job's son's house to collapse sweep through another part of town, taking even more lives? If so, the story of Job reminds us that large-scale disasters boil down to individual stories of suffering. And if God granted Satan permission to take away everything Job had, human logic would then also say that God is ultimately responsible for the pain of everyone else touched by natural and man-made disasters, for he allows it to continue. He may not have stirred up the Chaldeans to raid Job's camp, but he allowed Satan to stir them up.

He has a purpose in it all, we say. God will make good out of bad. He'll turn tragedy into something glorious. Saying this is much easier from a distance. In the epicenter, the words hollow out. Learning that God is in any way responsible (even if it is only because of his consent) calls into question everything we've ever heard about God. Loving? Kind? Gentle? How about cruel and heartless? Why doesn't God do something about the pain we endure? Why doesn't he stop injustice and the spread of disease? Why doesn't he do more good and stop more of the bad? If he can, why doesn't he?

This is the real problem of evil and the greatest stumbling block to accepting bad things from the hand of God. Something within us recoils against the idea of a good God allowing bad things to happen. Minor setbacks, maybe, and even personal handicaps and tragedies that serve to make us better people, we can accept. But we have to wonder if there isn't another way to accomplish the same purposes. Why must God use bad things in my life to accomplish higher purposes, if there is any purpose at all? Thoughts start bouncing in my head, thoughts of a choice I think I must make. Either God is cruel after all and I need to learn to accept it, or God is good but limited in his ability to stop evil. As we saw in an earlier chapter, the first is unthinkable. The second becomes more and more attractive as we experience suffering ourselves or as we try to help others survive their own personal nightmares.

One of the best-selling books of recent times on the subject of suffering chose the second option. In order to rescue God's reputation, to protect his image as loving and just and fair, the book concluded that God will not and cannot intervene either with the laws of nature or the freedom of humans to act in ways that produce destruction:

> Laws of nature do not make exceptions for nice people. A bullet has no conscience; neither does a malignant tumor or an automobile gone out of control. That is why good people get sick

and get hurt as much as anyone. No matter what stories we were taught about Daniel or Jonah in Sunday school, God does not reach down to interrupt the working of the laws of nature to protect the righteous from harm. This is a second area of our world which causes bad things to happen to good people, and God does not cause it and *cannot stop it.*[2]

The book builds on the premise that God doesn't lay specific burdens of suffering on anyone. Hearing the word *cancer* from a doctor does not fit into some overarching will of God. Rather, according to the book, these things simply happen to everyone. God doesn't cause them nor will he prevent them. Instead, the author asserts, he comforts and strengthens those who endure them.

A recent trend in Christian circles takes the same approach. Deemed the Open View of God or the Open View of the Future, this position teaches that God created a world with real freedom for its inhabitants—freedom God will not violate. Moreover, God took a huge risk in creating this world, for he does not know exactly what will happen. Events unfolding on earth are not foreseen or predetermined by God. Rather, this view teaches that all things simply occur as a result of the physical laws and human freedom God built into this system. God would do something about suffering if he could, yet the system he has created and the uncertainties of an unforeseen future keep him from doing so.

Proponents of this view believe that it offers the perfect solution to the problem of pain. God is absolved as innocent. According to this view, God is not the source of sufferings like those Job endured. He weeps with us when tragedy strikes. Horrific events like the Holocaust anger him. God doesn't orchestrate any kind of purpose behind them. Rather, he would like to eradicate such acts completely, and he wants us to join him in his efforts. Nightmares and tragedies do not fall under the will of God, nor are they part of his grand plan for creation. They simply occur. It is the risk he took in creating the world and the risk we take for living in it (as if we have any choice). Therefore, God remains loving and gentle and kind. He stands ready to give us strength as we suffer and to comfort us in our grief. Rather than becoming angry with God for our lot in life, we should be angry about the situations and injustices that cause our pain.

It sounds like the perfect solution and the perfect words of comfort to offer to those who hurt. There's only one problem: Removing God's ability to control the future and placing him at the mercy of the forces of evil downsize God. He becomes something far less than the God of the Bible. In the book of Job, we see God as the all-powerful Lord of the universe. The forces of evil do not have free rein to run around the earth, unleashing havoc wherever they see fit. Satan himself must stand before the throne of God to ask permission before he can strike Job. Nowhere in the book of Job or the rest of the Bible do we read that Satan must always seek God's permission before he can do anything, yet the insight into the courtroom of God shows us far more than a God who feels helpless to do anything about pain and suffering. God thundered forth in Isaiah 37:26,

> But have you not heard?
> It was I, the LORD, who decided this long ago.
> Long ago I planned what I am now causing to
>   happen.

Struggling with suffering leaves us wondering why God doesn't do something about our plight, yet jumping to the conclusion that he cannot creates more problems than it solves. We might find a moment of comfort in thinking a child's abduction and death took God by surprise and causes him as much pain as it causes us, yet it also leaves us with the stark conclusion that our pain doesn't have a point, and that's something we cannot live with. Every bad experience, every ounce of suffering we endure, becomes nothing more than the old form of torture where a prisoner has to dig a hole only to fill it up the next day. The next day he digs and refills it again. The cycle goes on and on, one pointless hole after another, until the prisoner finally goes insane. That's where a downsized God leaves us. We look for answers, but there aren't any to find.

When suffering hits, we do more than ask God why we have to go through this experience. We also begin frantically searching for something positive, some good that will ultimately come out of our nightmare. I'll never forget standing next to the coffin of an eight-year-old boy. His father stared vacantly down at his son, tears streaming down his face. "Since this happened," he told me, "a lot of people heard about Jesus who never would have listened. Everyone in town heard about what happened. They're even talking about it on the radio." He paused and looked over at me. "I just hope maybe that was the reason for this. There has to be a reason."

Reducing God to a helpless spectator, even a compassionate one, may make suffering more palatable, but it leaves it pointless. Yet suffering in the hands of a sovereign God does serve his purposes. I find this to be the most amazing aspect of God's power and plan. As we touched on in chapter 1, we live in a fallen world. Sin permeates every part of creation. Sickness and disease and death all resulted from Adam and Eve's decision to disobey God. Each of us follows suit. Every one of us is a sinner, and the end result of sin is death. In fact, the suffering that causes us the greatest grief, that causes us to question the existence of God, comes as a result of people's cruelty toward one another. I don't know anyone who ever became an atheist because a tornado ripped through town, but I know those who have rejected belief in a good God in a world where terrorists fly planes into buildings.

Because we live in a fallen world, suffering and pain and death will

25

always be present. Diseases will sweep across continents, wiping out huge portions of the population, and dictators will exterminate blocks of their people for no apparent reason. Yet none of these threatens to knock God off his throne. He doesn't have to stir up some pervert to rape and kill a child. Sin takes care of that. Yet the act neither surprises God nor derails his purpose and plan for each person's life. "I know the plans I have for you," the Lord said through Jeremiah (29:11). "For we are God's masterpiece," the apostle Paul wrote. "He has created us anew in Christ Jesus, so that we can do the good things he planned for us long ago" (Ephesians 2:10). God always remains in control, and he never changes.

Does this mean God wanted the Holocaust to occur? Of course not. Why, then, didn't he prevent it, and why doesn't he prevent other horrible things from happening to me and the people I know and love? The question assumes the Holocaust and similar acts of genocide simply arise out of thin air. They don't. The culture that produced the deaths of millions of Jews grew out of a tradition steeped in anti-Semitism. Martin Luther wrote the following nearly four hundred years prior to Auschwitz:

There are sorcerers among the Jews who delight in tormenting Christians, for they hold us as dogs. Duke Albert of Saxony well punished one of these wretches. A Jew offered to sell him a talisman, covered with strange characters, which he said effectually protected the wearer against any sword or dagger thrust. The duke replied: "I will essay thy charm upon thyself, Jew," and putting the talisman round the fellow's neck, he drew his sword and passed it through his body. "Thou feelest, Jew!" said he, "how 'twould have been with me, had I purchased thy talisman?"[3]

The Holocaust was the end result of a long history of hatred and violence that finally reached its zenith. As much as we want to see it as an aberration or the product of one madman taking a nation psychologically captive, it stands as a commentary on the human race. The fifteen to twenty million who died under Stalin in the former Soviet Union, the two million murdered by the Khmer Rouge in Cambodia, and the gruesome mass murders in Rwanda and other parts of Africa all testify to the unlimited potential for evil that resides in the human heart. For God to prevent all these things from reaching their logical conclusion would dictate removing the human race's ability to commit acts of evil. While on the surface that sounds like the perfect solution, such a radical act on the part of God would mean forcing all of us to do good. Our only choice would be to serve God, not as an act of love, faith, and worship but one of slavery. God has refused that option since the day he made the first man and woman in his image, for forced obedience brings him no pleasure. Like him, we have real choice, and God wants us to choose by faith to love him and obey him. As Hebrews 11:6 tells us, it is impossible to please God without faith. Unfortunately, the human race has chosen personal sovereignty over humbling ourselves before God and faithfully following his plan. Again, it is not as though God has left us in the dark as to how we can avoid the evil that plagues us. But from the beginning of time, human beings have chosen to ignore him. Along the way, we've refined cruelty to an art form, and we wonder why God allows it to continue.

I must then ask, Do these horrible acts of human cruelty serve God's purposes? At the risk of being misunderstood, yes. That is not to say that God in any way derives pleasure from death or injustice. However, part of God's judgment against sin involves allowing it to play out to its logical extreme. God gives the human race over to the choices we make (see Romans 1:18-32), and the consequences that naturally follow are then a part of his will. Does God want people to hate and murder and fight and engage in every form of malicious behavior? No. Over and over, by word and by the example of those who follow him, he's told us to do the very opposite. However, by "abandoning them to their evil minds" he lets the human race do things that should never be done (see Romans 1:28). You could then say that God wills those who refuse to acknowledge him as God to deteriorate into the basest of all behaviors. By doing so, the contrast between God's righteousness and the human race's decadence stands for everyone to see. Who could possibly mistake this temporary, physical world as any sort of paradise to be valued above all after looking back on the twentieth century or the short history of the twenty-first? Displaying his own glorious holiness against the backdrop of our utter depravity on the canvas of history serves God's purposes and draws people to his Son.

But what about tragedy on a smaller scale? Does it fit into God's plan? A few summers ago, I woke up on a Saturday morning with one goal in mind: to watch the British Open. When I turned on the television, golf was nowhere to be found. Instead, every network devoted all of its airtime to the unfolding story of the son of a former president whose small plane had crashed off the coast of Cape Cod. Intermixed in all the newscasts resounded one question: Why? Why would God, or Providence, or fate, or whatever or whoever is in control of the universe allow one more nightmare to envelop the Kennedy family? Why would God allow such a thing to happen?

At the risk of sounding insensitive, I have to ask what is to me the more obvious question: Why would God prevent this plane crash? Is it up to God to forcibly remove the keys to a plane from the hands of someone who is about to fly into conditions he cannot handle? Is it God's responsibility to temporarily suspend the laws of nature every time a member of the human race places his or her safety at risk? Is God to be the ultimate nanny, keeping us out of harm's way lest one of us strike our foot against a stone?

At times I wish he would. I wish he would prevent the germs that have taken up residence on a doorknob from taking up residence inside my body when I open that door. I wish he would prevent my triglycerides from skyrocketing when I overindulge myself with cheeseburgers and milk shakes. I wish God would become the ultimate safety net, protecting you and me from ourselves and from the fallen world in which we live. But that is a role he refuses to play, and he refuses for our sake. If he removed all the risk, all the tragedies, all the heartache from life on planet Earth, we would never long for anything more. We would never long for God.

When suffering strikes us personally or someone we love suffers, we often feel as though the situation is beyond God's control. The thought that he is helpless to do anything crosses our minds. That's normal. Yet, in some way we do not understand, God is in control. Nothing takes him by surprise or derails his plan for our lives. He will work through all things in such a way that he will be glorified in the permanent world of eternity. Knowing this allows me to accept every step of my journey with Christ, no matter how painful, as part of God's plan for my life. Without this assurance, we're left stranded in the dark. No hope. No peace. Nowhere to turn.

CHAPTER 11

BREAK POINT

Tomorrow will be different. Everything will be okay tomorrow. If I can just make it through today. Tomorrow. I just have to make it until tomorrow. Then I can catch my breath. Then I will see the light at the end of the tunnel. Then I know I'm going to make it. Today I'm not so sure, but tomorrow will be better. The pain will be more manageable. I'll have a clearer picture of what I need to do. Tomorrow. I just have to make it until tomorrow.

Then tomorrow comes. And it feels like today. Nothing has changed, at least not for the better. I still hurt. I still have to force myself out of bed. Tears flow far more often than I would like. The dull ache in my chest and the emptiness in the pit of my stomach won't go away. I think maybe I should go see a doctor, but I already know the diagnosis: stress. Try to alleviate your stress, he'll tell me, which strikes me as wildly hilarious. Try living stress-free with this pain that will not go away. Once it seemed funny. Now, though, I don't feel like myself. It is as though someone else has taken over my body, someone sadder, someone more cynical, someone I don't much care for. I had hoped I could get out of this someone's grip on me, but I can't. Not today.

Maybe I will tomorrow.

But there have been so many tomorrows since all this started. I never thought it could last this long. About the time I think it is over, about the time I think life will return to normal and I can get on with living, it all starts again. And the dull ache returns, and the emptiness and the sadness, and the stranger takes over my body. I never thought this could happen to me. I heard stories, but I always thought problems like this would confine themselves to other people. And then one day it was my turn. I didn't even realize I was in line. If I had, I would have run away. Now I can't. The longer it goes on, the fewer options I have. Every morning I feel myself being dragged farther and farther inside the dragon. I thought time would be my ally. Time is supposed to heal all wounds. But the longer this drags on, the more I realize the calendar is my biggest problem. It won't let go. It stubbornly refuses to give me back my life. Now I'm left count-ing the hours until tomorrow, hoping Scarlett O'Hara is right and tomorrow will be another day. She's probably wrong and I'm living *Groundhog Day.*

The suffering that pushes us to the breaking point is different for each of us. The trials may vary, but one fact remains: Following Christ does not exclude us from the pain everyone else in the world lives through. If anything, living by faith may actually increase the likelihood of pain and problems. From Abel dying at the hand of his brother to John writing the last book of the Bible while exiled on the rocky island of Patmos, the Bible is filled with stories of people who suffered as believers. Paul and Peter both remind us that everyone who wants to live a godly life will encounter trials and tribulations. All the problems we encounter, all the whirlwinds sweeping across the desert, all the raiding Sabeans, are complicated by one simple yet inescapable feature: time.

Because we can read the book of Job in one sitting, we sometimes think the events of the book cover a week or two. Job suffered intense pain. He accepted his lot even as he complained to God. A few days later, he rebutted his comforters and lived to enjoy the restoration of all he had before. Job encountered his worst nightmare and moved on to normalcy in what sounds like two weeks, maybe three. Yet it is far more likely that Job's disaster dragged out over months, perhaps years. Much of the pain stuck with him the rest of his life, even after his fortunes were restored. In some ways, Job's life probably never returned to normal.

They say time heals all wounds. Maybe it does. But first it picks at them, deepens their pain, drags them out until all our strength has failed. In reality it doesn't have to do anything to accomplish these tasks. All it has to do is pass. And pass slowly. Whether sitting in a waiting room or searching for a job after the position you held for twenty years was downsized out of existence, time drags when life hurts. Along the way, we go through many different phases, all of which take us to one inevitable place. Given enough time, we will all reach a breaking point.

It doesn't start that way. Mixed in the midst of the wild range of emotions we feel when suffering first strikes is a sense of resolve. We pray. We hope. We worry. But we feel determined to meet the challenge. Although we may break down and wonder how we will ever get through this, the conviction that somehow we will, that God will carry us through, keeps us going. We hear this kind of resolve from the lips of Job: "The Lord gave, the Lord took away, blessed be the name of the Lord" (Job 1:21). He didn't turn against God or charge him with wrongdoing. In all this, Job did not sin by blaming God.

The human spirit is so strong that most of us can accept a crisis as God's will for a day or two. But when the days turn into weeks and the weeks into months and the months into—you get the idea—we wonder how anyone can survive. Especially alone. When our world starts to fall apart and bad things appear to multiply day by day, a sense of isolation descends like a shroud. People may surround us, the phone may ring with calls of love and support, but we still feel alone. Part of our isolation is real, part imagined. People often back away from us when we're going through trials. They don't know what to say to us, and much of what they do say sounds irrelevant. Who wants to talk about last night's ball game when you aren't sure you will survive the day? I don't. Nor do I want to talk about the problem that envelops my life, yet I can't keep from it. A friend will ask how I am doing, and before I know it, more and more of my story spills out. I know she has to think I am losing my mind. The problem is time. It is taking its toll on me and my sanity.

As time goes by, we withdraw more and more. Suffering does that to us. We pull back in large part because we know that others do not really know what we're going through. This new experience of unimagined pain sets us apart. Others may say they know what we're going through, but unless they've walked the same path, they don't. They can't. Nor can they appreciate the magnitude of the emotions with which we wrestle. No problem ever looks as large or as menacing until it parks itself in your own living room. We hear the stories and they sound like things we would rather avoid, but we do not know how horrible they actually are until they strike us. We think we can imagine what it must feel like to lose a child or a spouse or a parent, but we can't — not until we experience the pain for ourselves.

If any of Job's comforters had ever buried a child, their words would have been entirely different. If they had awakened one morning to find themselves covered with boils, they might have been more compassionate, less quick to judge. They each felt free to share their great insights into the inner workings of God because they'd never found themselves on his wrong side. They saw the destruction in front of them. Their eyes absorbed the reflected light from the burned spot in the field where fire fell from the sky, and the broken remains of a collapsed house, and the oozing sores on their old friend, but they didn't comprehend the magnitude of what they saw. People on the outside looking in never do. They think we should get over our pain and get on with life. No wonder we feel so isolated, so alone. We're left to fend for ourselves.

As crises drag on, eclipsing months and stretching into years, we start to second-guess ourselves. We question all the decisions we made that led up to this point. "If I had only . . ." becomes the starting point of most of our conversations with those around us. Homes break up at this point. Careers get thrown away. We feel like we have to change something, anything, to get out of the mess we're stuck in. Hasty decisions rarely lead to lasting resolution. And time keeps marching on.

At some point we hit a wall. Our problem should have ended by now. Instead it compounds itself into a giant lint ball of death, rapidly adding new problems and new complications. About the time we think we have a handle on one set, another jumps up. Like a firefighter trying to put out a grass fire on a dry, windy day, we keep running from one problem to the next, trying to extinguish all the flare-ups. We find ourselves in a heavyweight boxing match. Mistakenly, we think the end of a round means the end of the problems. Calm comes, and about the time we think life is back to normal, the bell sounds. Time to get back in the ring. Only eleven rounds to go. Small problems creep in, problems that by themselves wouldn't even cause us to blink. Throw them on top of everything else we're dealing with and they feel like the final straw. And then our critics chime in. There are always people who feel they need to fill the role of Eliphaz, Bildad, and Zophar. They've watched us long enough; now they need to contribute their infinite wisdom to our problems.

The real problem is time. It keeps pushing, chipping away at our strength. We keep asking ourselves how much longer this can go on.

Unfortunately, the answer is far longer than we ever imagined. The eleventh chapter of the book of Hebrews, the great faith chapter, ends with stories of people whose trials never ended.

Others trusted God and were tortured, preferring to die rather than turn from God and be free. They placed their hope in the resurrection to a better life. Some were mocked, and their backs were cut open with whips. Others were chained in dungeons. Some died by stoning, and some were sawn in half; others were killed with the sword. Some went about in skins of sheep and goats, hungry and oppressed and mistreated. They were too good for this world (see Hebrews 11:35-38).

Time never let up, but they never backed down. Just when it seemed things couldn't get any worse, they did.

The longer problems persist, the more complicated they become. They don't simplify themselves or become more compact. Day after day they spread further, consuming more and more of our lives. If they would just come and go, we could handle them. Accept bad things from God? Fine, I can do that, if the bad things will line up single file and schedule themselves at appropriate and sensible intervals over a lifetime. When they don't, when they plant themselves in our lives and refuse to go away, when they multiply and diversify with each passing day, we find we can't possibly accept them as coming from God. "Why would he do something like this?" Job kept crying out. "Why won't God relax his hand from me, why won't he give me rest, if only for a day? Why won't this stop?"

Monotony compounds the fatigue. Every day feels just like the day before. We long for tomorrow, but tomorrow is a bad imitation of today and the day before. Regular routines disappear only to be replaced by a new routine we would rather live without. The days of the week lose their rhythm. They all feel like one long day that won't end. Fatigue sets in. Our minds cloud over. We can't think straight and we know we shouldn't make any decisions. Finally our strength gives out completely. We can't take another step; we can't live with this another day. We're broken. Finished. Time finally broke us, which is exactly what it was supposed to do.

Once we reach our breaking point, we discover that the tide does begin to turn. Even if our problems remain at full flood and our suffering doesn't go away, something snaps inside of us. We come to realize that this new reality is the way life will be from this point forward. If it will not end, we have to make a choice. Either we can keep on screaming at God and blaming him for our pain, or we can accept this new reality and get on with life. What we thought was normal may never come back. Longing for it only makes today harder to endure and tomorrow more disappointing. Instead of longing for a day that will never return, we must accept the day that now is. All our problems and their long-term effects are our lot in life. We can either accept them and move on, or we can sit down and complain and allow our lives to end now. The latter feels right for a while, but when time refuses to send us back to where we were before, we must choose the former.

That's why we have to reach our breaking point. That's why time keeps marching on and trampling us with every step. God knows we must reach the end of our strength before his strength can take over. He told Paul, "My grace is sufficient for you, for my power is made perfect in weakness" (2 Corinthians 12:9). When Paul's strength gave out, when he was left broken and weak and desperate, God could display his power with perfection. Unless Paul was broken, he never would have experienced the wonder of God's grace. God will push me to the very same point. This is what I now accept as God's will for me at this point of my journey with him. I don't just accept the bad things from the hand of God; I relish the sufficiency and perfection of his grace.

Accepting bad things from the hand of God is not an act of fatalism where I throw up my hands and sigh, lamenting, "There's nothing I can do." I can hit this point and give up and still miss what God wants to teach me. He wants me to learn that his grace is sufficient for whatever I go through. His power is all I need, not to escape my pain but to serve him and glorify him while I suffer. God's grace doesn't provide a way out; instead, it supplies all the strength I need in the midst of my pain. "My power is made perfect in weakness." In my moment of weakness, when my trials and pain threaten to overwhelm me and I feel my grip on the hand of God start to slip, God's power and grace shine in perfect glory. I can never put God's glory on display in this way when times are good. His power is perfected and his glory shines when time takes its toll and I cannot take another step in my own strength. That's the place God wants to take me. That's what it means to accept this part of the journey as God's will for my life. God's will is not that I suffer but that I display his power and his grace for all creation to behold.

I wrote that last sentence so quickly and easily that it may have sounded as though this is an easy thing to do. It is anything but. Nor is the process I described in this chapter an instanteous affair. In my own life, I've found it to be long and hard and messy. Some days I'm better at it than others. About the time I think I've accepted this new normalcy and surrendered it over to God, I find myself back at what feels like the beginning. But it's not the beginning. I've made further progress than I imagine because God is the one carrying me along. His strength is displayed in my weakness, and I find it to be most prevalent when I feel the lowest. Slowly, methodically, God brings me along when I let him do so.

CHAPTER 12

CRUEL

And now I start to sound like Eliphaz. I can't help it. As C. S. Lewis said, "All arguments in justification of suffering provoke bitter resentment against the author."[1] So let it begin. Let the accusations fly. "He doesn't know what he's talking about!" you shout, and you may be right. "What kind of pain and suffering has he ever gone through?" you yell at the page, and I have to admit that compared to what you face every day I probably haven't gone through much. That isn't to say I've lived a pain-free life. But suffering, like beauty, is in the eye of the beholder. When someone else loses a loved one we think, *How sad*, and go back to watching *Andy Griffith* reruns. We may shed some tears and send flowers or go to the funeral, but we escape largely unscathed by the experience. Put us on the other side of the room, plant us in the chairs reserved for the closest family members, and everything changes. The pain grows infinitely more intense because it belongs to us. In some ways we feel like the first and only people to have ever stood next to the funeral director picking out caskets. No one knows how we feel. No one.

And here I stand in the background telling you to accept your pain and suffering as gifts from God. Job never used the word *gift*, but he implied it when he put good things and bad on the same plane.

We must accept bad things in the same way we accept every other blessing from God, he tells his wife. Pain and suffering are blessings. They are gifts from God.

There. I said it. I called bad good. I pulled the oldest dodge in the book when it comes to pain and suffering and the presence of evil in the world by redefining it as good. Sorry. I didn't have any other choice. Telling you God sends suffering your way not because he hates you but because he loves you is not an attempt to sidestep "almost intolerable intellectual problems."[2] Nor am I trying to pull a Pollyanna and tell you to look on the bright side of everything. Job didn't say to look on the bright side or adopt a rose-colored perspective on reality. He told us to accept bad things from the hand of God for the same reason Paul told the church in Philippi, "You have been given not only the privilege of trusting in Christ but also the privilege of suffering for him" (1:29). Jesus did the same thing when he called the poor and sad and persecuted blessed by God (see Matthew 5:3-11). He went beyond Job by telling us to leap for joy when we are hungry and weeping and mocked and cursed (see Luke 6:23). I don't think the Savior was speaking metaphorically. Peter and James echo Jesus' words when they tell us to consider the wide range of troubles surrounding us as opportunities for joy (see James 1:2-4; 1 Peter 1:6-7).

And then there is this: "We know that God causes everything to work together for the good of those who love God and are called according to his purpose for them" (Romans 8:28). We've condensed it into the handy little saying "Everything will work out for the best," yet that isn't what the verse says. Everything will not work out one way or the other by itself. God is the one who works. He weaves together everything we experience, every moment of joy, each devastating heartache; all of them come together in his eternal purposes to bring about his good in our lives. I'm struck by the larger inference of the promise. God doesn't respond to unforeseen tragedies in our lives by trying to make something good out of them. He is not the ultimate "lemons into lemonade" maker. Instead, the verse and its context clearly imply that bad things happen within the framework of the work God is already performing in our lives. How this works is a mystery, for much of what happens in our lives is anything but good. Yet God demonstrates his majesty by working through everything, even the darkest of days, to accomplish his ultimate purpose in the lives of those who love him. He doesn't respond to the bad. An unforeseen tragedy does not cause God to scramble for some sort of plan B that will still take us to his ultimate destination for our lives. He knows all of the twists and turns our lives will take, both good and bad, and he has laid out his plan for our ultimate good through them.

The Bible resounds with this message throughout both the Old and New Testaments. God allows affliction and sorrow and hardship in our lives as a means of accomplishing the good work he wants to complete in us. Pain is not inherently evil. It is, in fact, a tool through which God accomplishes good purposes. Don't confuse this with looking on the bright side or making the best out of a bad situation. Making lemonade out of life's lemons focuses on trying to make something good come out of bad. In effect, it is to accept bad things by reshaping them into something positive. But that is not what I'm talking about. To accept bad things from the hand of God does not mean tolerating them until something good can be made out of them. Instead, we trust in God's wisdom with the hope that he is already working through everything, good or bad, to fulfill his higher purposes.

So what good is God trying to do that makes it necessary for him to make my life miserable?

If suffering did nothing more than cause us to hate this world and long for the world to come, that would be enough. The more we hurt, the more anxious we become for something more, something better, something not corrupted by sin. We long to go home and be with the Lord. But God longs for this even more. His Word speaks of a unique kind of fellowship we share with him in suffering (see Philippians 3:10), fellowship we cannot experience any other way. Trials also make us holy. Peter tells us that choosing to suffer for Christ means making a break with sin (see 1 Peter 4:1). Both Paul and James describe the road to maturity as leading through the land of trials and tribulations (see Romans 5; James 1). Without suffering we would remain spiritual infants. Suffering purifies our faith, refining it like gold in a furnace (see 1 Peter 1:7). Pain teaches us to rely upon the grace of God rather than our own strength (see 2 Corinthians 13).

All these benefits come as we suffer, not after suffering ends. The real giants of the faith are those who learn to accept hardships and suffering for Christ, even to the point of losing their lives. Suffering is more than a tool in the hand of God; it is one of the essential ingredients of the Christian life. Without it we will never grow in our faith or become mature in Christ.

Yet that doesn't explain why the anguish we go through must be so intense. I can understand how God uses disappointments and setbacks to purify my faith. Giving me everything I want leaves me spoiled and immature. I need months where bills outweigh my income as a way of teaching me to rely upon God alone as my provider. Simple tests, even though they don't seem so simple at the time, I can handle. But where is the benefit in Job-sized suffering? Telling me Job had to lose everything he owned just so God could make a point makes God sound cruel, especially when I think of Job's ten children. Why did they have to die? I know God causes all things to work together for good for those who love him and are called according to his purpose, but how can the deaths of ten innocent children be good? It all seems so extreme, so beyond any reasonable explanation. God may have a reason for doing something this severe, but it is hard to believe, especially in light of conversations like one I had last week.

One of my friends and his wife have been through a lot over the last few years. I called him because I wanted to find a way to use his story as an encouragement to others. After listening to the raw emotion in his voice, I reconsidered. Over the course of their marriage, Paul and June suffered several miscarriages, but losing the last child was the worst of the experiences. When Paul found out June was pregnant, he called and e-mailed friends across the country. His excitement was tempered by the fear five miscarriages naturally produce. "Pray she'll go full term," he asked. A couple of months into the pregnancy, everything changed. A test revealed the baby had Trisomy 18, which meant every cell in her body was genetically flawed. June would carry Hannah full term, but the baby would not survive more than a few days, maybe no more than a few hours. The doctor suggested they terminate the pregnancy. Paul and June couldn't. Both firmly believed that life begins at conception and every life is a gift from God. How, then, could they choose to end this precious life God placed in their hands? Thousands of people all across the country prayed for a miracle, but none ever came. The day Hannah was born was also her last. Trisomy 18 did exactly what the doctors predicted. Hannah never had a chance.

Shortly after Hannah's death, Paul walked away from the security of his job. Conditions there had never been ideal. His supervisors adopted new mission statements and business philosophies every couple of months, or so it seemed. Turmoil and tension filled the air as personnel turned over. Paul always put up with it as a necessary evil of the job, but under the weight of his grief, it became more than he could stand. His split from work was amicable, but running into people from the office still brings back unpleasant memories and anger. In this mix of uncertainty came a phone call about Paul's father. The two of them had a strained relationship while Paul was growing up. "I finally figured out my dad was just plain crazy," he told me. Now came the news that Dad had been diagnosed with Alzheimer's. His condition rapidly deteriorating, Paul would have to care for him. Other problems hit at the same time, most of which Paul couldn't even talk about. Together they scraped the scars off old emotional and psychological wounds. The weight of it all is more than Paul or anyone can handle.

Paul knows that God is in control. He knows all the verses about trials producing endurance and endurance producing character. He's heard people quote Romans 8:28 so much he can hardly stand it. When he talked to me last week, he said,

> And I keep thinking that if all of this is necessary in the eyes of God, I feel like not so politely telling him to leave me alone. Hearing that God has some sort of plan doesn't make him seem gracious. It makes him sound cruel. I know I shouldn't think this way, but I look at the hand God has dealt me and I want to yell at him, "I deserve better than this!" I know we all deserve death and hell; that's not what I'm talking about. You know, I've dedicated my life to God, I strive to live a life of integrity, I've made hard decisions for him and stuck with them even when it would have been easier to go the other way. And this is what I get. I keep thinking I should get something better.

My friend is angry with God, and here I stand trying to tell him bad is good in the hand of God. It sounds cold, heartless, and cruel. Here's the real struggle we have in trying to accept bad things from the hand of God and allowing him to take us through anything and everything to accomplish his good purposes. The trials he drags us through are not just simple tests of faith; they are destroyers of lives. I started writing this book after three of my friends in different parts of the country had their lives devastated by different trials all in the span of six days. How can I walk up to any of them and tell them that God causes all things to work together for good and not sound like a cold heartless jerk? Should I go up to Rebecca, whose mother lost her three-year fight against cancer, and tell her to leap for joy in her time of mourning? Maybe I'll drive down to see my friends whose son died alone on a hillside when his four-wheeler flipped over on top of him and tell them to let this trouble be an opportunity for joy. They're already trying to do that, and maybe they will succeed some day. For now they can't even go into their dead son's room. They closed the door the day he died, and no one has entered since. How can I talk to any of them about the positive aspects of suffering without making their anguish seem trite and God seem cruel?

I can't. When pain is intense enough, the Bible verses we quote to offer comfort don't sound compassionate. Just listen to one of my favorites: "What we suffer now is nothing compared to the glory he will give us later" (Romans 8:18). *The New International Version* reads, "I consider that our present sufferings are not worth comparing with the glory that will be revealed in us." I love the promise of that verse. God has something so glorious waiting for us in heaven, something so beyond description, that our suffering on this earth will seem like nothing in comparison. The very memory of the worst this life throws at us will fade as we bask in the glory God will give us later. How can we stay down? How can we help but leap for joy? This is not just good news; it's great news! That's how the verse sounds when we struggle with the normal trials and pain we encounter as we walk through life.

Then I try to hear the verse through my friend Paul's ears. He still wrestles with grief and thoughts of what might have been with the child he buried. Every day he cares for a man whose memory of him is quickly fading away, a man who made Paul's life miserable as a child. And then there are other problems, troubles he couldn't bring himself to share with me. He feels crushed beneath their weight as though he cannot catch his breath. Just about the time he feels that the burden is about to lift, he sees God throwing something else on the pile. Romans 8:18 says to Paul, "What you suffer now is nothing compared to . . ." The rest of the verse fades out, or if it is heard at all it sounds like this: "You won't get any relief until this life is over." Paul knows the promise is true, he's just not sure he can wait that long. He needs relief today, now. He prays for this pain to end now, but Romans tells him he must keep carrying it. And, by the way, in God's eyes his lot in life doesn't look so bad. "Your trials are nothing," the verse says.

God's promises do sound cruel. That doesn't change the fact that they are true. God never explains why life must be so harsh, but we shouldn't be surprised that it is. Jesus told us we would have trouble in this world. Now when it strikes us, we face a choice: We can choose to believe that this present suffering is part of God's plan that will ultimately result in good, or we can stay mad at God the rest of our lives. It is not an easy choice to make. Anger comes naturally when people hurt us. When God is the one handing out the bad, we can hardly help becoming angry with him. Again, this doesn't change the fact that his promises are true. He does have a purpose. He does have a plan. Accept it, Job tells us. It's a privilege, Paul tells us. Rejoice in it, Jesus tells us, with Peter and James shouting, "Amen to that!" Now we have to choose to see it this way.

PART THREE

COULD GOD HAVE SOME PURPOSE BEHIND ALL I'VE BEEN THROUGH?

And I am sure that God, who began the good work within you, will continue his work until it is finally finished on that day when Christ Jesus comes back again.

—PHILIPPIANS 1:6

CHAPTER 13

WHERE MY FUTURE LIES

"So are you writing anything new right now?" Tim asked me as we trudged through the weeds, trying to get to the far end of the cross-country course in time to see our daughters run by. Not only did our daughters run together, they spent nearly 90 percent of their free time at one or the other of our homes. Even though Tim's daughter and one of my three had been best friends since the first grade, Tim and I didn't get to talk very often. His life stayed busy between two teenage children, his job with a major pharmaceutical company, and caring for his wife, who lost all use of her arms and legs in a car wreck several years earlier.

"Yeah," I answered, "I'm working on a new book. In fact, my deadline's just a few weeks away. I hope I make it."

"What's the book about?" Tim asked.

I refrained from launching into a mini-sermon. Our daughters would come running out from a group of trees at any moment, and the conversation would change into cheers and shouts. I decided to give the simplest answer possible. "Suffering," I replied.

"So have you ever suffered?" Tim's answer shot back so fast it caught me off guard. My mind raced over all the things I thought were bad when God sent them my way. Walking through the high weeds with this man, nothing I'd experienced looked too bad.

"Not like you have," was all I could say as I pulled a thistle out of my sock. Frankly, I was a little embarrassed. How could I compare the minor struggles of the past few years with the serious challenges his family has been facing?

Tim and I talked a little longer as we stood and waited for our daughters to emerge from the cornfield on the back of the course they call "The Beast." I didn't mention this section of the book. I found it a little hard to jump right into all the good things God wants to do through the bad things that come our way. Who knows, it might have been a good field test for this book, but I didn't want to sound like Eliphaz.

I didn't want to sound like Eliphaz to Tim, and I don't want to sound like him to you, either. As you and I go through sufferings, we have God's promises that he can and will work through them. He gives the assurance that he will accomplish his purposes through trials and work for our ultimate good. Yet there is one thing God's promises will not do: They will not make pain become less than pain, grief become less than grief, and suffering become less than suffering. God's promises give us the hope we need to survive, but they don't make the unbearable bearable. In fact, I don't think we can really understand the specific ways God works in our individual suffering until the pain diminishes and life settles into some sort of new routine. In the midst of troubles, we usually can't see how God is at work. Even if he stood right in front of us and waved his arms, saying, "This is my reason for allowing your life to blow up in front of you," I don't think our minds could process the information. The middle of the nightmare isn't a good place to insert the moral of the story.

That's not what I'm trying to do.

Nor do I mean to downplay the trials you face. Far too often that's the impression well-meaning people give when they try to tell us all the good God can accomplish in the bad we're going through. It's as though we say, "Wow, your husband walked out on you and your three young children; that's really bad. But don't be sad. God's gonna use this somehow. Now, don't you feel better?" God may use whatever you are going through in ways you cannot possibly imagine today, but that doesn't make the situation any less horrific. As I come alongside you and encourage you to accept bad things from the hand of God, I'm not telling you your trials are inconsequential. Your pain is real. Your troubles are bad.

That's how Jesus saw it. One day he received word that one of his close friends was sick. Rather than rush to his house and per-form a miracle, Jesus waited several days. He waited long enough to ensure that his friend was dead. Then he went to see him. When Jesus arrived at the home of the deceased, his friend's sister came to him with tears streaming down her face. "Master, if you had only come when we called for you, my brother would be alive right now."[1] His friend's other sister didn't say anything. She stayed near the grave in numb silence. Her grief so overwhelmed her she couldn't cry or yell or scream at Jesus for not showing up on time. She just sat and stared. Jesus didn't come in time to heal his friend because he planned to do something even more amazing. He planned to raise a man from the dead who'd been buried four days in dry, arid heat. When he told the people near the tomb to roll back the stone, they objected because the smell would be so rank. But that comes later in the story.

Before Jesus ordered the stone to be rolled back, before he arrived at this house in Bethany, before he received word his friend was sick, Jesus knew the story would have a happy ending. The man in the grave would walk out, people would be amazed, and God would be glorified. Even though Jesus knew all of this when he arrived on the scene, he stopped and wept with the two sisters. He didn't tell them they were wasting their tears. Nor did he tell them to rejoice because

God had arrived. Even though all of that was true, he didn't trivialize his friend's sisters' grief. Instead he cried with them.

God is already at work in whatever bad situation you face today. His plan for your life continues to unfold, and he will not be deterred until it is completed. He made a promise, and he will keep it. But the pain still hurts. The grief still feels overwhelming. You still wonder why God must be so unfair. Clinging to his promise doesn't take that away, nor should it. Pain must hurt. Suffering must ache. Bad things from the hand of God must always feel bad. The moment they begin to feel bearable and normal and not so bad, we may easily fall back into relying on our own strength rather than upon God to work in our lives.

Tim's question still rings in my ears. Have I suffered? Definitely not as much as Tim and his family, and probably not as much as you, but please, don't tune me out. Pain within the soul serves the same purpose as the pain I feel when I put my hand on a hot stove. When the flesh on my palm starts to burn, I know I need to move my hand away from the stove as quickly as possible. Pain in my soul does the same thing. Yet rather than forcing me to remove myself from the source of my pain, it moves me to turn to the source of my hope. Listen to the words of David, the ancient king of Israel:

> Have mercy on me, LORD, for I am in distress.
>> My sight is blurred because of my tears.
>> My body and soul are withering away.
> I am dying from grief;
>> my years are shortened by sadness.
> Misery has drained my strength;
>> I am wasting away from within.
> I am scorned by all my enemies
>> and despised by my neighbors —

even my friends are afraid to come near me.
When they see me on the street,
    they turn the other way.
I have been ignored as if I were dead,
    as if I were a broken pot.
I have heard the many rumors about me,
    and I am surrounded by terror.
My enemies conspire against me,
    plotting to take my life.
But I am trusting in you, O Lord,
    saying, "You are my God!"
    My future is in your hands. (Psalms 31:9-14,
        emphasis added)

David's prayer expresses more than blind resignation to the pitfalls of life. He hasn't surrendered to the trials of life. Nor does he try to pretend that the pain that wracks his body does not exist. But his tears and pain and distress are not the end of his story. "I am trusting in you, O Lord," he cries out, "my future is in your hands." This is what it means to allow God to work in and through whatever you are going through right now. Though our sight is blurred by tears, we believe that God is there. And into his hands we place our future.

CHAPTER 14

WEANED FROM THE WORLD

The squirrels in the walls finally put us over the edge. When they wouldn't move out, we decided it was time for our family to go. It wasn't as if we loved the house to begin with. Neither my wife nor I ever thought we would live there until retirement, anyway. The squirrels just hurried the process along.

We lived in a parsonage, and for those unfamiliar with the joys of parsonage living, suffice it to say it's a lot like living in a rental property with your employer as a landlord and volunteers with varying skill levels serving as the super. The church bought the house cheap a few years earlier, and the craftsmanship inside showed why. Part of the attic had been converted into a room, and even though we were more than a thousand miles from the nearest ocean, it always made me a little seasick. I think it may have had something to do with the way the walls bowed in and out like waves. The kitchen floor funneled down toward the corner next to the stove, which came in handy when the roof leaked. And the roof leaked a lot, especially during the winter after a good, heavy snow. Gallons of water regularly piled up in one corner, making it easier to suck up with a Shop-Vac. And I do mean gallons. One night I stayed up and filled a five-gallon bucket twice with melting snow that dripped onto my stove. This came after volunteers from the church replaced the roof.

The kitchen floor joists were too small and too far apart, which caused everything on the kitchen table to shake violently when our dachshund ran by. The basement leaked, which wasn't too bad except the drain didn't work, but even that wouldn't have been that big a deal except that the hot water heater sat flat on the basement floor. The morning after a big rain we would wake up to discover we didn't have hot water because the lake in the basement had snuffed out the pilot light. I hated going down to relight it because the only way to reach it was to lie on the wet floor, although doing so helped keep the bats who lived in the basement from hitting me in the head. Going down there when the lights went out, searching in the dark for the box and the right fuse in it, wasn't quite as fun. Standing in water unscrewing fuses while ducking bats left a lot to be desired. Sometimes the bats came on up into the house itself—not too often, just every spring and fall. My wife and our three daughters never warmed up to the bats. My girls usually screamed bloody murder and ran to the garage when a bat came inside, leaving me to play tennis with it. The bats always lost, and eventually they left.

Then came the squirrels.

The squirrels never lost. They never left.

No one in the family ever actually laid eyes on a squirrel. The exterminator told us we probably had a piney squirrel or a chipmunk in our walls, based on the size of the pellets he found in a crawl space. Whatever they were, they sounded like acrobats, not squirrels, especially above my daughter's room. It was on one end of the part of the attic converted into a room. The squirrels liked to get into the ceiling and run relay races from one end to the other every night about the time our daughter went to bed. We tried everything short of dynamite to get rid of them. Live traps, poison, a snarling dachs-hund, even boom box CDs cranked up to eleven with the speakers directly next to the squirrels' last known location. Nothing worked. When the squirrels grew tired of the attic, they went up and down the inside of the walls of my room. They usually waited until midnight to start that.

I tried conquering the squirrels for well more than a year. Whenever I began to think I had prevailed, they'd come back. We all reached our breaking point the night a squirrel took a wrong turn inside a wall, wedging himself in a strange position. He began flailing and scratching and squealing, trying to free himself. The entire wall became a sort of echo chamber, magnifying the noise and the creepy factor at the same time. I had only two choices: Take out a twelve-gauge shotgun and begin blasting away at the walls, or give the parsonage to the squirrels and move out. We chose the latter. It was an easy choice to make. After all, the house didn't belong to us. None of us ever mistook it for our dream home. While we lived there, we were thankful for it, but squirrels and bats and leaks and everything else wrong with the house kept us from wanting to stay any longer than we had to.

The causes of the pain and suffering we encounter in this world are a lot like the squirrels in the walls of that parsonage. Neither will ever be eradicated. Hurricanes will blow and floods will rise and blizzards will howl as long as time goes on. Earthquakes will shake California while tornadoes skip across Oklahoma. The economy will go up and down while companies go bankrupt and jobs disappear. Cars will wreck and planes will crash and every new technology will come with its own set of risks. Bones will always break because acci-dents will always occur. People will always get sick. And everyone dies in the end. We may be able to postpone the latter by cutting back on fried foods or reducing stress levels (by, say, moving out of a house with squirrels in the walls), but we can never change the fact that every person will eventually die. Watching loved ones pass will always fill us with grief. Walking away from their gravesides will never become a pleasant experience.

Life will never seem fair. Good people will die too young, and evil people will appear to dance through life unscathed. The powerful will oppress the weak while justice sometimes goes to the highest bidder. Crime will not end; neither will poverty. Wars will be fought and people will die as a result until the end of time, and there's nothing we can do about it. We may be able to stop a war here or reduce tension there, but the war to end all wars came a couple of dozen wars ago. This is life. There's nothing we can do to change it. We call life fair when the war stays on the other side of the globe or someone else's father fights for his life in the ICU. Suffering begins when the bombs go off in our backyard or we sit beside the hospital bed amidst all the tubes and wires.

Like I said, it's life and it operates exactly according to God's plan. The world in its original state didn't include grief and suffering, but God designed creation in such a way that this system we hate came into being the moment the first man and woman tried to trade places with God. Now this fallen world serves God's purposes, although it doesn't bring him pleasure. All the suffering and all the pain and all the injustices in the world work on an eternal scale to accomplish the same goal the squirrels had when they moved into my house: They make us want a new home. If God removed all the pain and troubles inherent in this fallen world, we would remain content living here forever. No one would ever step back from life and say, "Is this it? Is this all there is?" Instead, we would be satisfied living separated from God in a world corrupted by sin.

The writer of the book of Ecclesiastes had everything his heart could desire. Money, power, fame, women, pleasure — he had it all.

Yet one phrase rolls through the book: "Everything is meaningless, life is meaningless." What caused him to reach this conclusion? Listen to his words: "Then I said to myself, 'This is all so meaningless!' For the wise person and the fool both die, and in the days to come, both will be forgotten" (2:15-16). The writer of Ecclesiastes took an honest look at the world around him, and this is what he saw: He watched people work hard all their lives only to die before they could enjoy any of it. In another corner of the city, he heard the cries of the oppressed, but no one came to their defense. He saw sickness and death and people scratching for food but never finding enough. Good people died young; evil people lived long and healthy lives. In short, he saw the real world, a world of pain and suffering and death. "Here is my final conclusion," he wrote. "Fear God and obey his commands, for this is the duty of every person" (12:13). He understood that God uses the worst things in this world to turn us to him. Until we get disgusted with this world, we will not look to God.

In 1886, the French government gave the United States a gift celebrating the one hundredth birthday of American independence. The copper statue, designed by Frédéric Auguste Bartholdi and placed on Bedloe's Island in New York Harbor, soon became the symbol of an open door to the persecuted poor of Europe and beyond. At the base of the statue are inscribed these words penned by Emma Lazarus of New York, a Jewish relief worker who established her standing as a poet and translator:

> Give me your tired, your poor,
> Your huddled masses yearning to breathe free,
> The wretched refuse of your teeming shore;
> Send these, the homeless, tempest-tost to me,
> I lift my lamp beside the golden door.

Royalty and aristocrats didn't walk away from their lives in the old world to risk everything on a new start in a strange place. Only the desperate came. They came fleeing persecution or famine or a hopeless life. America's population grew out of the huddled masses, the desperate.

The same holds true of those who long for new life in God. Jesus said it is easier for a camel to squeeze through the eye of a needle than for the rich to enter heaven. Time has shown his words to be true. When he walked this earth, only the sick and the poor and prostitutes and outcasts followed him. Those with nothing had no problem with his demand to leave everything behind to follow him. But the rich didn't respond. They listened to him for a while, but they found his demands too radical. Their comfort kept them from seeing their need for Christ. Nothing has changed in two thousand years. The comfortable ignore Christ, the desperate flock to him. What choice, then, does a loving God have but to allow life to become unpleasant in order that we might see our need for him? If possessions and good health and a comfortable career keep us from even thinking about questions of eternity, shouldn't God take those things away in order that we might see our need for him?

Does that mean God would allow someone we love to die in a horrific accident simply to get us to notice him? I don't really want to answer that question, because I am afraid you will misunderstand what I need to say. Before I answer, let me say again: We live in a world where people die every day in all sorts of ways that strike those left behind as horrible and cruel and unfair. And they are horrible and cruel and unfair. Death is always an intruder for those created in God's image. However, because we live in such a world, the question is not whether God would allow an accident to strike someone we love. Instead, the question is, can such an accident derail God's plan? And the answer to the latter is no. But what is more amazing to me is the way in which God takes that which is horrible and cruel and unfair and works within it to accomplish a work in our lives that we may never have embraced otherwise. The suffering inherent in life on earth goes beyond opening our eyes to our need for God. It shows us how fleeting and ultimately worthless everything this world has to offer really is.

The world in which we live will soon pass away. John wrote, "This world is fading away, along with everything it craves. But if you do the will of God, you will live forever" (1 John 2:17). His words show the world as a whole, including all its priorities and systems, to be exactly like the individual parts. Everything we strive for, everything the world considers to be important and permanent, lasts no longer than that sort-of-gray T-shirt in my closet that used to be black. Everything wears out, fades away, and will one day cease to be. Even if it were possible that Jesus never returns to earth, the natural processes God built into nature would eventually destroy it. The sun will one day burn out or blow up and life on earth will cease. The universe itself will stop expanding and will naturally collapse back onto itself, ending life even on a microscopic level. Yet the Bible says God plans to intervene long before that could happen. Jesus will return to establish his reign upon the earth. Before he ushers in eternity, he will create a new heaven and a new earth. The earth on which we now reside will be destroyed by fire as the final vestiges of anything corruptible are removed forever.

"Don't store up treasures here on earth," Jesus tells us, "where they can be eaten by moths and get rusty, and where thieves break in and steal. Store your treasures in heaven, where they will never become moth eaten or rusty and where they will be safe from thieves" (Matthew 6:19-20). If everything on this earth is temporary, we're wasting our lives pursuing any of it. Cars break down, carpet wears out, plaster cracks on the walls in one-hundred-year-old houses. Every day a great deal of our time is spent trying to keep back the forces of decay. Moths and rust ultimately get everything anyway. Why waste our time? Material possessions always leave us disappointed. And even if our stuff does last, we won't. A Louis XIV desk or a Tiffany lamp may be worth a lot of money on the *Antiques Roadshow*, but Louis XIV and Tiffany aren't here to reap the benefits. If they had been able to take them with them, the *Roadshow* would have nothing to show.

Not only does suffering shove this truth in our faces, it forces us to make a choice. We can either pursue things that will not last, or we can lay up treasures in heaven. By allowing this temporary world to overflow with sickness and death, God makes the choice easier for us. And we have to choose. As much as we would like to deposit treasure in heaven and enjoy it here on earth, we cannot. "No one can serve two masters," Jesus told his disciples. "For you will hate one and love the other, or be devoted to one and despise the other. You cannot serve both God and money" (Matthew 6:24). We will either pursue God and his purposes for our lives, or we will be devoted to this world and all it can offer. The two are going in opposite directions. Suffering shows us which one matters and which does not.

It still strikes us as a little unfair, or perhaps excessive. Surely God doesn't have to go to these extremes to get our attention. The world is passing away and everything in it. I understand. But does he have to rub it in our faces? Does he have to make this life so distasteful and bitter? I think he does. The human race has a way of adapting to any environment. Though we crave luxury and comfort, we find a way to make the best of any situation, even behind bars. A few years ago, I met a man serving a life sentence in a prison outside San Diego. He stood apart from the rest of the prisoners. Well educated and formerly wealthy, he didn't commit a crime of passion or throw his life away on drugs. No, this man earned his life sentence out of boredom. Life as a computer software executive hadn't given him the kick he wanted, so he hacked into sensitive government files and created havoc. Time behind bars hadn't affected him, at least not on the surface. "How do you stand it in here?" I asked. "Don't you miss your old life?"

He paused and looked down for a moment before answering. The morning sun warmed our backs. He raised his head and pointed off in the distance. "Nah, this place isn't so bad. Look, I can still see the ocean from here. It's not too bad." I doubt whether he would refuse parole if the state of California offered it to him, yet he wasn't throwing himself up against the razor wire begging to get out. He adjusted. This was his life and he planned to make the best of it. If he ever did get out, I doubt if the horrors of prison would keep him straight. He'd lived there. He'd adjusted. It wasn't so bad.

God has something better than this world in store for us. In Matthew 16:26, Jesus asked, "How do you benefit if you gain the whole world but lose your own soul in the process? Is anything worth more than your soul?" Of course not. If we have everything but lose our souls, we really have nothing. Nothing the world can offer is worth the price of eternal separation from God. Through suffering we learn that the opposite is also true. When we lose the whole world but gain our souls, we discover we have a real bargain. When the world becomes more than unpleasant, when it wears us out and makes us completely sick of its decay, we begin to realize that the only thing we really want is heaven. Trials and suffering have a way of making this truth come alive in a way nothing else can.

As long as this world remains palatable, we won't want anything else. When the pain increases, when the ugly reality of life on earth becomes more than we can bear, our souls long for something more, something permanent. Deep in our hearts we ache for God and God alone. He weans us from the world in order that he might give us the gift of himself.

CHAPTER 15

DISCOVERING GOD IN THE MIDDLE OF MY PAIN

Desperation has a way of stripping everything down to its essentials, and when life turns bad, our one essential becomes God. With all our heart, mind, soul, and strength, we seek him and plead with him. We pray more. We cling to his promises more. This closeness born of despair doesn't fit the stereotype of an experience with God. It's not all smiles and joy and hallelujahs and tingles running down the spine. We don't even realize how close God is until the crisis passes. In the middle we often feel alone. Very, very alone.

We are never closer to God than in times of trouble, but I don't know anyone who is eager to take this statement to its logical conclusion. No, most of the people I know who claim to love Jesus talk about how when times are good they will stick near him. From reading the Bible to praying to going to church, we try to stay close to him; we really do. But life always seems to get in the way. The job and the family take so much of our energy, we fall asleep when we try to read a chapter or two of Ephesians. The family schedule keeps getting tighter. One child needs to go to art lessons while the other has basketball practice. We struggle just to eat one or two meals a

149

week with everyone at the table at the same time. Carving out time to spend alone with God would be great, but we can hardly find five minutes for ourselves. Once or twice we tried to turn drive-to-work time into prayer time, but it didn't work too well. The yard needs work and so does the house. Can we help it that Sunday is the only day we have to get things done? When we do make it to church, we try to keep anything from distracting us from our pursuit of God, but without realizing it we keep glancing at our watches, wondering when the service will be over and we can get on with our day.

At the end of the week, we look back and feel guilty about how little time God actually had our full and undivided attention. We can hear him calling, but the noise of life yells louder. The Spirit of God pulls us one direction while life yanks us in the other. Undeterred, God pulls a little harder by making life less attractive. He wants to do more than pry our fingers off of things that don't last. He wants us. All of us. Our whole heart and soul and mind and strength with nothing held back. In times of suffering he gets us. At long last we find time to pray without ceasing. Our desire becomes fixed upon God, even if it's only the desire for him to fix the mess we're in. Whatever our motives, we finally turn totally toward God. Put us in the dry and weary land where our spirits feel parched and we will cry out with David in Psalm 63, "O God, you are my God; I earnestly seek you." When tears become our food and discouragement fills our souls, our souls will thirst for God (see Psalm 42). God gets all of us with nothing held back when bad things fall down on top of our heads.

And God meets us there even when we don't realize he's there. Life starts to hurt, so we run to God only to find he's already running toward us. There are times when the moment is unbelievable. We cry out and God responds. His grace sweeps over us in a way that feels as if we could open our eyes and see God standing next to us. Those are the moments we never forget. However, and this is one of the hardest *howevers* with which we will ever come to grips, usually the fellowship we experience with God during times of suffering does not feel like a particularly religious moment. In fact, it feels like nothing at all—nothing except pain and loneliness and all the other emotions we pray God will take away. God does not invade our space with an emotional experience, nor does he send that special someone our way with just the right words we need to hear right when we need to hear them. Occasionally he does, but more often than not we are left to go on faith alone. His promises are all we have to pull us through. They don't necessarily run through our minds, yet they are there. We find ourselves praying without saying a prayer. We hope without thinking about the object of our hope. In the heat of the moment, we don't even think about God, yet after the moment passes and we look back, we find we have gripped his hand tighter than ever in our lives. And we understand that not only was he with us, we found ourselves closer to him than we've ever been before.

Reaching this point can be a real struggle. We long for the divine experience. We want to feel the shivers running down our spines and the comfort of his touch. When God takes them away, we think he left with them. He didn't. The less I feel of God, the harder I have to believe, the more I must pursue him. What I've often mistaken for a dry spell is instead the richest time of knowing God. He didn't feel close. My emotions remained untouched. All I had was God's assurance that he would not leave me or forsake me. But really, what more do I need?

That's God's goal. He wants us to know him more. To know God means more than increasing our knowledge of facts about him or having emotional experiences with him. God wants us to develop intimacy with him that transcends understanding. Through trials, God takes what we know in our minds and hearts about him and brings it to life. As he does, we move from knowing the promises of God as words on a page or a feeling running down our spines in a worship service. We truly experience God himself.

One of the great promises God gives us is found in the eighth chapter of Romans. Listen to Paul's words:

> Can anything ever separate us from Christ's love? Does it mean he no longer loves us if we have trouble or calamity, or are persecuted, or are hungry or cold or in danger or threatened with death . . . ? I am convinced that nothing can ever separate us from his love. Death can't, and life can't. The angels can't, and the demons can't. Our fears for today, our worries about tomorrow, and even the powers of hell can't keep God's love away. (verses 35,38)

I know this promise is true because God included it in his Word. But when I come face-to-face with death and the fears of today and worries about tomorrow, the promise is more than spiritual truths on a page. It becomes the place I meet God. I feel the weight of trouble and calamity and hunger and cold trying to pry me away from God. Waves of doubt sweep over me. Strange thoughts race through my mind as I wonder why God, if he loved me, would put me through such garbage. Anger wells up inside of me. And sadness. And despair. Through the torrent of emotions, God reaches down and pulls me to his side as I remember his Word. In that moment, I experience truth. I know experientially that nothing can separate me from Christ's love, because I live it. As a result, I come to know God in a way I never did before, in a way I could not before my life fell apart.

This is the bottom line of everything we go through in this life, good and bad. God gave his Son in order that people like you and me might know him personally. He doesn't just want to drop tickets to heaven in our back pockets or give us peace and happiness in this life. We miss the point when we think in these terms. God had one purpose in creating us, he has one purpose in saving us, and he has one purpose in taking us to heaven when we know his Son as our Lord and Savior. He wants us to know him intimately. We confuse facts and feelings with true knowledge of God. He doesn't. Throughout the Bible, he compares the relationship he chooses to have with us to the relationship enjoyed by a husband and a wife. When Jesus returns, he comes as a bridegroom coming for his bride. Call it a hunch, but I doubt that the key to a successful marriage is the ability to spout a few facts about another person or sharing an occasional e-mail.

God wants to share our lives, and he is willing to do whatever it takes to make this a reality. Our sin separated us from God, making any kind of relationship impossible between the two of us. God removed our sin and bridged the gap between us by giving his Son as a sacrifice for our sin. Heaven and earth are still far apart. God came near to us by planting his Spirit within everyone who trusts in Jesus alone for their salvation. How could we know any of this unless God told us? So he did, through his Word, the Bible.

When we still find the world too much of a distraction from seeking God, he will at times break its hold on us through trouble. I do not mean to imply that this is always the purpose God wants to accomplish through the bad things that come into your life, but it often is. We treat God like a life jacket in our fishing boat, so God lets our boat spring a major leak in the middle of Lake Superior. Why God would accept us under such circumstances is a mystery. But he does. And he will continue to use the bad things of life to draw us closer to himself and to develop an intimate relationship between us as long as this life endures. There is a fellowship we encounter with him in suffering we cannot find any other place. The moment doesn't always feel sweet, but it leaves us changed. Forever.

The way in which God uses pain and suffering to enhance our relationship with him does not stop there. God doesn't just draw near to me and share my sufferings. He wants me to share in his. Paul put it this way: "As a result, I can really know Christ and experience the mighty power that raised him from the dead. I can learn what it means to suffer with him, sharing in his death, so that, somehow, I can experience the resurrection from the dead!" (Philippians 3:10-11). "I can learn what it means to suffer with him," Paul wrote. What on earth is he talking about? We know that Christ suffered in the past when he walked on this earth. Religious people harassed him; ordinary Jews rejected him and, ultimately, crucified him. As Paul carried the gospel throughout the Roman Empire, he experienced similar reactions. He was whipped, flogged, beaten with sticks, stoned, and left for dead. By suffering for the gospel, Paul suffered like Jesus. But Paul doesn't say he can learn what it means to suffer in the same way Jesus suffered. He talks of sharing Jesus' suffering now. In some way, Paul seemed to believe he shared in Christ's present sufferings, as though the suffering of God did not end on the cross.

As we suffer, we come to experience the heart of God, who suffered and who continues to suffer. That's part of a real relationship. So often we settle for a one-way street, where God comes to our aid, makes us feel better, and fixes our situation. We don't have to think about how he feels. All we care about is ourselves. But God, who wants to share our lives, also wants us to share in his. He wants us to feel what he feels, to see the world through his eyes and with his heart. This fallen world inflicts pain on God, but not in the sense of a powerless being suffering under circumstances he cannot change. Far from it. God is God, the Lord over all the universe. Yet his Word makes it clear his heart still breaks over events on earth. He wants us to share those feelings.

He wants us to share the grief he feels over those who die without him.

He wants us to feel the pain of rejection he receives from a world that tries to act as though he doesn't exist.

He wants us to feel the heartbreak of loving someone unconditionally only to have that love trampled upon.

He wants us to know the sacrifice of choosing to lay aside our right to get even and instead freely offer forgiveness.

How do we know that God wants us to share his heart? We see it in his Word, especially the Old Testament prophets. God told the prophet Hosea to marry a prostitute. The request sounds odd. I don't know many churches anxious to hire a pastor whose wife was and continues to be a hooker. Apparently, God didn't care. He told Hosea to marry a prostitute named Gomer, bring her into his home, love her, and have children with her. There was only one problem. Gomer didn't want to leave the red-light district. She didn't love Hosea. Even after they married, she kept sleeping with other men. It was a marriage made for the *Jerry Springer* show. Hosea didn't know which, if any, of their three children was his. Eventually Gomer left him and went back to her street corner. God told Hosea to go find Gomer, forgive her, and keep on loving her. Only then would his prophet know the pain God felt every time his people rejected him for idols made of wood and stone.

God isn't pulling the divine equivalent of a child yelling, "Now you know how I feel!" His goal is to build a relationship with us. Healthy relationships depend on both parties coming to know one another's hearts. We grow closer as we think less and less of ourselves and more and more of the other person. God already became flesh in order that he might share our weaknesses. Now, through suffering, he wants us to discover the wonder of what it means to feel what he feels and see what he sees in the world. I think of my friend who lost his son in a tragic accident. He found comfort in the fact that God, too, watched his Son die, and it forever changed the way in which my friend reads the story of Jesus dying on a cross. Whereas before he always viewed the scene from below, as one of the multitudes for whom Jesus died, he now sees the cross from above. He knows experientially what God felt as he watched his Son die. I have to be honest: I hope I never gain that insight.

When we suffer, we not only experience God's love, we also learn more of his heart. We learn experientially of his faithfulness to his promises as well as begin to see life through his eyes. Sharing suffering with God knits our hearts closer together. It moves us along from immature children who need constant reassurances of God's love to mature adults who walk by faith without any evidence. God wants to know us personally and intimately. He longs for our relationship with him to grow every day. If it takes suffering to make that desire a reality, he will allow it. He loves us. What other choice does he have?

CHAPTER 16

DOES THE ROCK ENJOY BEING CHISELED INTO A STATUE?

"Have you ever heard of something called Awana?" Jim asked me. I expected him to tell me about his son or daughter on the outside attending the children's discipleship program. But he didn't. "I went to that Awana thing when I was a kid," Jim continued. "Yeah, I really liked it." He took another drag on his cigarette, his right leg propped on top of a trash can, his left continually bending and straightening as if he were trying to loosen up for a race. Not that there was anywhere to run. The yard of the Trustee Unit of the Indiana State Prison in Michigan City, Indiana, was smaller than a grade-school playground. Eighty percent of the yard lay in shadows cast by the walls of the main prison. A few clumps of grass poked up sporadically, but most of whatever wasn't covered in concrete was bare ground. And there was a lot of concrete along with fences topped with razor wire. Prisons always have a lot of razor wire.

Jim asked me about Awana because he knew why I came to the prison. He'd already heard whatever I had to say. He had heard it as a kid in church, and he didn't want to hear it again. The Awana clubs introduce children to Christ through games, Scripture memory, and Bible lessons. It's a wonderful program. By the time a child finishes sixth grade, he or she will have memorized several hundred verses. Jim didn't stick with it through the sixth grade. For whatever reason, he drifted away from Awana and church by the age of ten or eleven, yet he still remembered a little of what he heard back then. The program at least got his attention.

"I learned a lot of Bible in that Awana thing," Jim went on. "Seems like we got little prizes for all the verses we could say." He smiled. "Kids still wear those vests?" he asked. I nodded that they did. He went on, "Yeah, I kinda liked it."

"Did you believe what Awana taught you about Jesus?" I asked. Not taking anything for granted, I quickly inserted a brief summary of how people can be saved through Christ.

"Oh sure, I believed all that God stuff, at least I did at the time," he replied as he flipped his cigarette butt onto the grass. "I even tried Jesus when I was a kid. Didn't work though. Didn't keep me out of trouble." He paused. "I even tried it again when they stuck me in here the first time. 'Course, it didn't keep me from getting in trouble again." Jim lit up another cigarette while he switched and began stretching his left leg. "I don't think I'll try God again."

Our conversation stalled at this point even though we talked for another ten minutes. I kept talking and he listened, but we both knew he was just being polite. Nothing I could say would convince him he needed Jesus in his life. He'd already been exposed to Jesus and God and church and the Bible. And he remembered some of it. A handful of the Bible verses he memorized to earn stickers were still with him—not all of them, but enough to convince him that he already knew everything I had to say. He tried Jesus as a child and again as an adult, but nothing about God or the Bible kept him out of trouble.

Or out of prison. He finally decided the whole God thing didn't work and he walked away.

Jim's not alone. Ten years ago in his book *Exit Interviews*, William Hendricks reported that 53,000 people leave churches across North America and Europe each week and never go back. "To put that in perspective, consider that the United States lost about 57,500 people in the Vietnam War. In a different sense—though strangely appropriate—the church 'loses' almost that many every week."[1] Barna Research Group findings bear this out. In 1991, 24 percent of all adults were unchurched; that is, they had not attended a church service outside of a wedding or funeral in the past six months. By 2002, the number jumped to 34 percent.[2] Not even the tragedy of 9/11 affected the numbers. American churches experienced a brief spike in attendance immediately following the terrorist attacks, but within a few weeks, the numbers returned to their pre-9/11 levels.[3]

People walk away from church and God for a variety of reasons, yet many are just like Jim: They leave because God didn't work for them. Faith. Jesus. Church. None of it did what they hoped. I wonder what Jim expected God to do in his life. Did he think praying the prayer on the last page of the Four Spiritual Laws would somehow cause the prison system to give him an early parole? And did he believe that once he was back on the streets God would protect him from future arrests? Jim believed his life would somehow be different when he called out to the Jesus he remembered from childhood, but how different? After spending half an hour with him, I walked away with the impression that Jim primarily wanted Jesus to make his life happier. He wasn't all that concerned about major changes in his attitudes or actions. Sin didn't bother him. His primary desire was to feel better about life and about himself. When God didn't deliver, Jim went off in search of another source of happiness.

Jim walked away disappointed because God isn't nearly as

concerned about making us happy as he is in reshaping our lives in the image of his Son. Once we entrust our lives to him, he sets out to reproduce the character of Christ in us. Paul captured the essence of Jesus' character in his letter to the church in Philippi: "Though he was God, he did not demand and cling to his rights as God. He made himself nothing; he took the humble position of a slave and appeared in human form. And in human form he obediently humbled himself even further by dying a criminal's death on a cross" (2:6-8). When we think of Jesus, we think of one who surrendered his will to the will of the Father even though it cost him his life. Although fully God, he refused to use his divine rights. Instead, he emptied himself and became completely dependent on the power of the Father as revealed through the Holy Spirit. He also emptied himself of dignity and allowed himself to be humiliated as he hung naked on the cross. "He did not retaliate when he was insulted. When he suffered, he did not threaten to get even. He left his case in the hands of God, who always judges fairly" (1 Peter 2:23).

People come to Christ hoping he will make their lives better, and he does. God invests in us the rest of our lives, working on us and in us for our ultimate good. He doesn't waste his time on something as trivial as personal comfort. No, God aims much higher. Because our greatest good lies in him, he works to systematically remove the vestiges of sin left within us. Slowly, painfully, he remakes us so that his image in us might shine. We don't jump into a crash course in self-improvement. God does the work, not us. Over time, he performs a complete personal makeover from the inside out. His plan is to empty us of everything that marked our old way of life when we lived in rebellion against him. In its place, he wants to fill us with the character and passion and faithfulness of his Son. The process is not easy, nor painless, especially when we fight against God by holding onto the favorite parts of our old way of life. Peter described the process like this: "Since Christ suffered physical pain, you must arm yourselves with the same attitude he had, and be ready to suffer, too. For if you are willing to suffer for Christ, you have decided to stop sinning. And you won't spend the rest of your life chasing after evil desires, but you will be anxious to do the will of God" (1 Peter 4:1-2). God reproduces the character of his Son in us as we share in the sufferings of Christ. Hebrews 2:10 tells us, "In bringing many sons to glory, it was fitting that God, for whom and through whom everything exists, should make the author of their salvation perfect through suffering." Jesus was made perfect through suffering. Why would we expect anything less in our own lives?

If Jesus was made perfect through suffering, we are in effect asking God to make our lives less pleasant when we ask him to make us more like Christ. Jesus said, "People need more than bread for their life; they must feed on every word of God" (Matthew 4:4). We sometimes forget that he said this after fasting forty days. What better way could God choose to imprint this same truth on our souls than to allow us to experience physical want? God is opposed to the proud but gives grace to the humble (see 1 Peter 5:5). What greater gift, then, could he give than the gift of humility? Jesus taught us to love our enemies and pray for those who persecute us. Isn't he simply giving us an opportunity to put his words into action when he allows difficult people to surround us? I don't want to go hungry or be embarrassed or put up with jerks. In fact, I'd rather do just about anything else, but I know I need difficult circumstances to empty me of myself in order that I might be filled with Christ.

Saying we want to be closer to God and more like Jesus is easy; actually making our desire reality can never be anything but painful. Overcoming the sinful desires at war in our soul comes through crucifying our flesh and surrendering our will to the will of God. Jesus said, "If any of you wants to be my follower, you must put aside your selfish ambition, shoulder your cross, and follow me" (Matthew 16:24). In the Roman world, people carried a cross for only one reason: to die on it. The little I've read about crucifixion tells me it was a horrifically painful way to die. Jesus chose these words to convey to us the painful process we will have to go through to be finally free of sin. Each day we pick up our cross means another putting to death of the sinful desires inside us. As Paul said, "Put to death the sinful, earthly things lurking within you" (Colossians 3:5).

God uses physical pain and suffering to help us do this. In the previous chapter, we explored the way suffering makes this fallen world disgusting in our sight. John tells us not to love the world or the things in the world. The more unpleasant this world becomes, the easier it is to fall out of love with it. God uses the same process to break the grip sin has on our hearts. Peter said that those who choose to suffer for Christ decide to stop sinning. In effect, suffering sets us free from sin. This isn't automatic. People can use a sudden downturn in their lives as an excuse to go off the deep end. Yet pain and suffering in the lives of Christ's followers can make it easier for us to crucify the flesh and follow Christ with single-minded devotion.

Suffering also produces strength of character within us. Jesus suffered his entire life. Isaiah predicted the Messiah would be a man of sorrows, one intimately acquainted with grief. All through Jesus' ministry people made threats against him. Many times he scavenged for food as he traveled from place to place, yet the deprivations he experienced throughout his life enabled him to endure the ultimate act of suffering when he died on the cross. By submitting his will to the will of the Father even when it caused him discomfort and pain, he was prepared to obey even to the point of dying a criminal's death on a cross. Here's how the writer of the book of Hebrews described the scene: "He was willing to die a shameful death on the cross because of the joy he knew would be his afterward" (12:2).

Just as Jesus was made perfect through suffering, God perfects his character in us through pain and trials. Troubles produce spiritual stamina. Lying around the house sipping Pepsi doesn't prepare anyone to run a marathon. If it did, you would see me at the front of the pack in Boston every year. The process of training, of pushing yourself to your limits, breaking down muscles to build them back stronger, always hurts. That's why I don't run. I can't stand the pain in my legs and the ache in my chest. I prefer the couch. One of my daughters can run circles around me. I may be able to take her in a quick sprint because my legs are longer than hers, but if we run any distance at all, I fold as she leaves me in the dust. Maybe it has something to do with the fact that she runs several miles every day, topping off the week with a five- or eight-mile run every Saturday. Over the course of the summer, she'll log between 250 and 300 miles. She has endurance because she is willing to put up with the pain.

God builds spiritual stamina in us the same way. He takes us through difficult times to build us up, to stretch us to our limit, in order that he might make us stronger. With time the tests become more difficult. They have to if we are to keep growing. God doesn't do this because he wants to torture us; he pushes us because he knows what lies ahead. We are in a spiritual war. Walking with Christ means living at odds with the world. Just as the world hated Jesus and put him to death, it will hate everyone who follows him. As if that weren't enough, God left us here with a job to do. He laid on you and me the responsibility of completing Jesus' mission and taking the gospel to the world. A task so large requires incredible strength and endurance. What we think is difficult today, the times when we think God has forgotten us or pulled something cruel against us, may not compare to what lies ahead.

The prophet Jeremiah discovered this when he complained about the burden God laid on him. Jeremiah found himself fighting an uphill battle. God called him to be his spokesman, yet no one would listen. They mocked him, destroyed his writings, even threatened his life. One day Jeremiah snapped. "How long are you going to keep doing this?" he complained. God gave him a straight answer: "If racing against mere men makes you tired, how will you race against horses? If you stumble and fall on open ground, what will you do in the thickets near the Jordan?" (12:5). If you think this is bad, he says, just wait. It's going to get much worse. Trials and pain today prepare us for the difficult roads that lie ahead.

Jeremiah didn't ask the next logical question, but I will. Why does the road have to be difficult? Why can't it be easy and trouble-free? Wouldn't people find the gospel more attractive if it resulted in an easier, more prosperous life? It might, but for all the wrong reasons. God would become little more than a means to an end. Those who came to him wouldn't want him or his Son. All they would really want would be the free stuff God handed out. Jim enjoyed Awana because his leaders gave him stickers and patches. Once he became too old for stickers, he thought he was too old for God.

Life isn't easy and trouble-free for anyone. Everyone experiences pain and grief and heartache. Everyone faces problems. Everyone gets sick. Everyone dies. If God somehow exempted his followers from trouble, how could we ever make him known to those who hurt? It's not just that we wouldn't be able to relate to them. No, something even worse would take place. We would never even notice those who suffer. It's not until we find ourselves sitting in the waiting room outside an ICU that we think about the pain others sitting there must feel. Even if we could force our eyes to see those who hurt, we couldn't relate to them. We wouldn't know what their pain feels like. All of our answers would be nothing but hollow words. How could we say that God will carry them through their suffering if we've not had to rely on him to carry us?

I think that may have been the biggest reason Eliphaz, Bildad, and Zophar, Job's comforters, spoke to him as they did. It wasn't that they lacked concern. As far as we can tell from the book, no one else even wanted to get close to Job. Most people were too afraid a stray bolt of lightning might hit them if they got too close. These three men alone made the effort to come and sit with their friend and try to comfort him. Their encouraging words did more harm than good, not just because their theology was bad but because their perspective was skewed. It is easy to talk about how God blesses the righteous when all you've ever experienced is blessing. You grow to assume that God will always act this way and that in some way you deserve it. But if one of Job's friends could have traded places with Job for an afternoon, his advice would have been completely different.

We experience calamity just like everyone else who lives in this fallen world, yet because of the hope we have in Christ, there is one distinctive difference. God uses suffering to implant in us the same compassion that flowed through Jesus. In his first public appearance, Jesus declared:

> The Spirit of the LORD is upon me,
>   for he has appointed me to preach Good News
>   to the poor.
> He has sent me to proclaim
>   that captives will be released,
>   that the blind will see,
>   that the downtrodden will be freed from
>   their oppressors,
>   and that the time of the Lord's favor has come.
>   (Luke 4:18-19)

He came to preach to the poor by being born into poverty. Outcasts found mercy in him because he himself was an outcast. We never find Jesus talking about locking up prisoners and throwing away the key. As he proclaimed freedom for captives, he knew that he, too, would one day share their fate. He didn't separate himself from those in need; instead, he became one with them. Jesus never even owned a home, much less one in the suburbs. He chose this life because of the compassion he felt for those who hurt. When he took on flesh two thousand years ago, he came not to end all suffering in this world but to share it.

Now Christ wants to continue to share people's suffering through us. Paul called him "the source of every mercy and the God who comforts us. He comforts us in all our troubles so that we can comfort others. When others are troubled, we will be able to give them the same comfort God has given us" (2 Corinthians 1:3-4). Real compassion and tender mercy characterized Jesus when he walked this earth. Now God wants these same character qualities to overflow from our lives. Living a painless, trouble-free life in which our every wish comes true will never produce character. Compassion for those who suffer comes as we live through the experience ourselves.

The character of Jesus can be reproduced in our lives only when we share in his sufferings. This isn't exactly what most people look for when they think of turning their lives over to God, but God would never settle for giving them anything less. First he has to empty us of ourselves. As Augustine said, "God wants to give us something, but cannot, because our hands are full—there's nowhere for him to put it."[4] Suffering empties our hands by emptying us of ourselves. Only then can God finish the work he wants to do in our lives.

CHAPTER 17

A PURPOSE THAT GOES FAR BEYOND THIS WORLD

Something still troubles me. We started this book with the story of Job and the question he asked his wife after his world collapsed. I understand that God uses our suffering to refine our character, but what did Job gain from his experience? Most of the benefits we've talked about, Job already had. He was godly, a man of integrity. God himself commented that no one in the world compared to Job in terms of righteousness. Although Job was rich, the world didn't have much of a hold on him. He freely shared with those in need. He didn't make decisions based on what was best for him. He fought for justice and stood up for the oppressed. When one looks at Job's life, he almost comes across as too good to be true. He was wise, faithful, fair. Even though his comforters accused him of leading a double life, they didn't have any evidence. They just assumed he must be a horrible sinner after his children died. In Job, people came face-to-face with one who treated all his servants fairly, fed the hungry, and cared for orphans and widows. He used money as a tool but never put his trust in it. He opened his home to strangers, loved his enemies as himself, and freely admitted when he was wrong. What was missing that God had to go to such lengths to produce?

I can't find an answer. Job's character had already been refined, so no more fire was needed. He didn't need more suffering. The world never had a grip on him, so no grip needed to be broken now. His faith didn't need to be purified. Even if it did, the depths of his suffering go far beyond making him a stronger believer. He lost everything. He didn't just suffer; his life was destroyed. God had to have a reason for allowing Satan to hit Job so hard, yet none of the passages that talk about the effects of suffering really applies here. Job already possessed endurance and integrity. His question to his wife that started us on this journey shows the magnitude of his spiritual maturity. Even when he lost everything, he continued to praise God's name. Again we have to ask, *What did Job lack that demanded God act in such an extreme way?* I can't find anything.

Does that mean Job's suffering in the book of Job was pointless? Hardly. Our suffering, like the rest of the Christian life, isn't just about us. The work God does through the suffering of his children goes far beyond the character development of one individual. He operates on a much larger scale that cannot be confined by time or space. God did not allow Job to lose everything in order that Job might learn that all he really needed was God. Job already knew that, but he wasn't the intended audience. In fact, the real reason Job lost everything had nothing to do with any event or person on earth. Satan accused God of bribing people into loving him. "Job only serves you," Satan sneered at God, "because you made him rich." God allowed Satan to destroy Job's life not just to prove the character of Job but to shut Satan up. By allowing Satan to attack Job, God launched a counterattack against Satan. Satan accused God of buying people's affections; God responded through the character of Job. When Job clung to the

Lord in spite of his material losses and personal pain, in spite of his fear that God had turned against him, God's point was made and Satan was silenced.

When we try to figure out the exact reason God allows us to suffer, we can drive ourselves crazy. We look at the people around us and wonder if God wants to use our pain to touch them. Whatever our pain may be, "If just one person can be spared," we will say, the ordeal will be worth it. At least our time wasn't wasted. We look inside ourselves for answers, turning over every part of our lives looking for the places God wants to change us. We ask God what he is trying to teach us, and we hope he answers us soon. No one wants to drag out suffering. We want to learn our lessons and get on with life. But nothing frustrates us more than going through a seemingly pointless ordeal. When the anguish drags on and there doesn't seem to be any reason whatsoever, we feel like giving up. Yet we may well be looking on the wrong plane.

Like Job, you and I are on display before both angelic and demonic powers. Paul put it this way: "Sometimes I think God has put us apostles on display, like prisoners of war at the end of a victor's parade, condemned to die. We have become a spectacle to the entire world—to people and angels alike" (1 Corinthians 4:9). The spectacles Paul described took place in large amphitheaters in cities scattered throughout the Roman world. Yet these theaters, some seating more than twenty thousand, weren't used only for entertainment. Rather, they served as large assembly areas where the men of the city gathered to debate issues. First Corinthians 4:9 tells us that we live in the middle of a celestial arena, where we are watched not only by the people around us but also by the entire heavenly host. We don't supply the evening's entertainment, with angels cheering on one side and demons on the other. The two sides debate, and we are God's evidence. Our actions, especially our reactions to trouble and pain, are the means by which God speaks to the gathered assembly.

Every day, good times and bad, our lives demonstrate the patience and kindness of God (see 1 Timothy 1:16). The angels can't understand the concept. They've never experienced the joy of forgiveness or the wonder of grace. The forces of evil find their tongues sticking to the roofs of their mouths in silence as they watch condemned sinners receive salvation. They want to yell, "Unfair!" or accuse us to God's face. They can't. In the center of the spectacle stands the cross, and hanging off the side of it, fluttering in the breeze, is a list of all the charges against us. Colossians 2:14-15 says that God took this list "and destroyed it by nailing it to Christ's cross. In this way, God disarmed the evil rulers and authorities. He shamed them publicly by his victory over them on the cross of Christ." Not only does our salvation reconcile us to God, it is also the means by which God defeated the forces of evil once and for all.

But the hardest evidence for the gathered assembly to comprehend is the patient endurance of those who love God. Satan and his minions watch us struggle with pain and grief and suffering. They wait to hear us curse God to his face. When they hear instead, "The Lord gave, the Lord took away, praise the name of the Lord," they have nothing to say in response. Every time a follower of Christ patiently accepts pain and suffering because of the hope we have in Christ, God extends the victory of the cross through us. "They have defeated [the Accuser] because of the blood of the Lamb and because of their testimony. And they were not afraid to die" (Revelation 12:11). Just as Job's did, our hope and endurance silences Satan and glorifies God.

That doesn't mean Satan ever gives up. God defeated him once and for all on the cross of Christ, but he keeps on fighting. Ephesians 6:12 tells us, "We are not fighting against people made of flesh and blood, but against the evil rulers and authorities of the unseen world, against those mighty powers of darkness who rule this world, and against wicked spirits in heavenly realms." Jesus put the powers of darkness to shame when he walked out of the grave alive. Now they've set their sights on us. Every day we are engaged in a spiritual battle, but it is unlike any fight the world has ever seen.

Some people want to portray spiritual warfare as some grandiose display where we bind the powers of darkness and take demonic forces captive. They speak of all the weapons at our disposal and the ways we wield them. You can almost hear the guns blazing and mortars blasting. But the book of Ephesians doesn't tell us to load up our spiritual M16s and pull an Arnold Schwarzenegger. We fight, and win, by simply standing firm. "Put on all of God's armor so that you will be able to stand firm against all the strategies and tricks of the Devil. . . . Use every piece of God's armor to resist the enemy in the time of evil, so that after the battle you will still be standing firm" (Ephesians 6:11,13). Stand. Resist. The Enemy plots strategy and pulls tricks. We stand. And we pray. "Pray at all times and on every occasion in the power of the Holy Spirit," Paul writes in verse 18. Outside of putting on God's armor, these are our only commands. Stand. Resist. Pray. A strange way to fight a battle indeed.

This is exactly how Job responded when he found himself in the middle of a spiritual battle. Demons didn't swoop down around him. Job never saw Satan the Accuser draw his bow, yet we know from the first two chapters of the book that all of Job's troubles had a satanic root. Satan accused Job of being a fraud and he suggested ruining Job's life. Behind the raiding Sabeans and Chaldeans we see the Devil, stirring up the world against Job. He even had the bright idea of covering Job with boils. This was spiritual warfare at its sharpest pitch. And how did Job fight back? He praised the Lord's name in spite of his intense grief. He accepted this turn of events in his life as readily as he accepted the blessings God sent his way. We read of his grief and the depths of his pain, yet we also read of a man who continues to stand and resist.

Job never rebuked the Devil. He never stood on a bluff overlooking his property while shouting Scripture at the forces of evil. His primary means of fighting this battle came in holding fast to God even though he was afraid God had turned against him. Satan went down in flames as Job remained devoted to the Lord. "Curse God and die," Job's wife urged him. Job refused. "You speak like a foolish woman," Job replied. "Should we accept good things from God and not bad?" In that moment, Satan lost. Job didn't have to fight back. He just needed to stand. The character of one godly person and his faithful response to suffering silenced the Devil and showed the futility of his efforts on earth. Satan thought he could turn people against God by making their lives miserable. God showed him that the power of his grace is so great that people will believe without any tangible benefit, a concept the Devil can never understand.

Does this mean our suffering has a demonic root? Not necessarily. All suffering and pain are a result of the presence of sin in the world. We live in a fallen world where everyone dies and grief and heartache run rampant. Trees fall over when they die and the base rots away. The Devil doesn't have to push one over for it to hit a car traveling by at forty miles an hour. That's just the world in which we live. Demonic forces also do not have to be personally involved when evil strikes us. The world is fallen because sinners live here. As long as sinners populate the earth, there will always be plenty of sources of evil and pain, even without direct demonic involvement. That's not to say that Satan may not be behind the trouble that strikes your life. He may be, just as he was in Job's life, but we'll never know unless and until God decides to let us in on the rest of the story.

Yet suffering for believers does not have to have a demonic root to play a role in spiritual warfare. The charges Satan leveled at Job continue to reverberate today. Cynics still charge followers of Christ with choosing the easy path. Karl Marx called religion the opiate of the people. I have an agnostic friend who sees Christianity as the easy way out of wrestling with the hard problems of life. Living in America, it is hard to argue with his position. Following Christ is easy in a country where no one persecutes us for our beliefs. The fastest-growing Protestant churches all sit in or near growing suburban communities, and the best-selling books tell us how to get more of God's blessings. Would we continue to follow Christ if God stopped the blessings and our lives became harder, not easier? Satan said we wouldn't. God bribes us into believing, the Devil charged in the book of Job. He isn't calling our character into question or accusing us of taking the easy way out. No, his finger is pointed directly at God.

Yesterday I watched a woman sit beside her husband as he inched closer to death. The doctor didn't expect him to live through the night three nights ago. The woman and her daughter never leave the hospital room. The man doesn't know they are there. Alzheimer's slowly took him away from them over the past three years, but his body remains and it fights for life with everything in him. The family requested no heroic measures be taken to prolong his life. He wouldn't want that either. Now they sit and wait for the inevitable. As I sat in the hospital room with them yesterday, I kept thinking I needed to leave. I didn't belong there. Any visit, even for a minute or two, is too long when a woman has to watch her husband inch closer to death. We talked about this book. I didn't bring it up; the woman's daughter did. She wanted to know how much I wrote that morning. I was embarrassed to sit and talk about something so inconsequential. I'd stepped into a very personal moment where I did not belong.

Yet so much more was taking place than I could see with my eyes. Amidst the grief and the pain was victory. The woman, her daughter, and the man fighting for every breath were quietly winning a spiritual battle. No one cursed God for this turn of events. No one shook a fist toward heaven and declared, "No one's there." Here they stood toe-to-toe with the ultimate weapon that sin can wield, and they were undeterred. They prayed. They waited. And they stood their ground, firm in the conviction that this man inching closer to death would very soon walk through the gates of heaven. The woman and her daughter might never be the same because of their loss, yet they continued to cling to the hand of God. Without realizing it, they fought and won a battle by their faith when not believing would have been easier than believing.

When you and I continue to hold fast to Christ when tragedy strikes, we answer Satan's charges and silence the spiritual critics. In effect, we replay Christ's victory on the cross and once again defeat the forces of evil. Peter put it this way: "Dear friends, don't be surprised at the fiery trials you are going through, as if something strange were happening to you. Instead, be very glad — because these trials will make you partners with Christ in his suffering, and afterward you will have the wonderful joy of sharing his glory when it is displayed to all the world" (1 Peter 4:12-13).

The suffering we go through makes us partners with Christ in his death, with the same result. Jesus died to disarm Satan and destroy the power of sin and death. Not only do we share in his victory on the cross when we turn to Christ by faith but we expand his victory as we continue to entrust our lives to him when all reason and logic tell us we're wasting our time. Someday soon all the battles will be over and we will have the joy of sharing his glory when it is displayed for all the world to see. May that day come quickly.

CHAPTER 18

TOE-TO-TOE WITH OUR
GREATEST ENEMY

I need to start this chapter with a confession. The title isn't accurate. I should have called it "Toe-to-Toe with *My* Greatest Enemy." We all have spiritual tests we feel God gives us over and over and over and yet we never really get it right. Welcome to mine. I wrote another book that explored slaying this enemy in great detail, in part in the hope that penning it would end the struggle. It didn't. If anything it only exacerbated it. C. S. Lewis once called security "the mortal's greatest enemy."[1] I cannot get his words out of my head. Late at night, as I lay in the dark worrying, once again earning a failing grade as my faith is tested, I hear Lewis whispering these words in my ear. Security is the mortal's greatest enemy, he says, and I am more mortal than I can bring myself to admit.

You needed to hear my confession so that you will understand the true tone behind this chapter. This is not a lecture. Nor am I talking down to anyone. If anything, I wrote this chapter for myself and myself alone. When I first penned it, I thought I had already conquered this battle. I felt confident in my ability to lean upon the Lord as my only source of security. Of course, at that point in my life, the memory of earning regular paychecks from a regular job remained fresh in my mind. I had quit my day job to pursue my nutty dream of becoming a professional writer a few months earlier, but the full impact of that decision had yet to be felt. Those months have now become years. And now for the crazy part, at least it sounds crazy to me. Since leaving my day job to pursue what I believed to be God's plan for my life, God has come through in ways I never imagined possible. Yet here I am, six years later, still struggling to trust God alone as my one source of security. Yes, "security is the mortal's greatest enemy," for anything that claims to be secure is nothing but an illusion in an insecure world. I can pretend the world is otherwise, until trials and suffering barge in unannounced and uninvited and turn my world upside down. Only then do I realize how my greatest enemy has me in his hold. I have to be honest: I don't like flying without a net. I don't like being forced to depend on that which I cannot see, and trust in that which I cannot feel around me. Colossians 3:3 tells me that my real life is hidden with Christ in God. That means that true life, my life that lasts, my only life that matters, is not affected by the uncertainties of life on planet Earth. My true self rests in God alone in heaven with Jesus. Therefore, I do not need to rely on anything in the world of time as my source of security, as my rock and anchor that I can lean on when life gets tough.

Here's the problem: I have trouble living what I know in my head. God may be my strength and my shield, but that regular paycheck was pretty nice even though I was miserable in my job at the time. Jesus may be my only hope, but knowing that my health is good helps me sleep at night. I call on the Lord, but I lean on my wife and family. All I need is what I can find in Christ, yet he's not all I depend on. I find my security in my stuff and my bank account and my ability to work and my health and my family and the country in which I live and the smoke detector that keeps me from dying in a fire at night.

Security is the mortal's greatest weakness, and I'm very mortal. So are you.

I never realize how much I'm leaning on something other than Christ until my other sources of security are threatened or taken away. And I don't want them to be threatened. When I listen to my prayers and the prayers of those around me, much of our faith in God revolves around hoping he will prop up the things we depend on other than him. Bills fill my mailbox; I ask God for money with which to pay them. One of my daughters goes off to the other side of the world on a mission trip; I pray that God will protect her. An unexpected pain wakes me up in the middle of the night; I ask God to heal it. Sadness fills my heart; I ask God for comfort and joy. Terrorists attack our nation, shattering our sense of safety, and we pray that God will quickly destroy our enemies. In between I ask God for clothes and food and shelter and a job and everything I need to make it in this world.

But what if I ask God for the money to pay my bills, and I lose my job instead?

What if I pray for God's protection over my family and my country, and disaster strikes?

What if I ask God to heal a pain, but the doctor has to pause and clear his throat before he can bring himself to give me his diagnosis?

What if instead of comfort I receive sorrow, instead of safety I'm plunged into a sea of uncertainty, instead of food and clothes and shelter, I'm forced to go around hungry and destitute and homeless? What if instead of propping up everything I lean on for security in this world, God allowed it to all slip away? If all or any of this happened, I would find myself in Job's shoes. But even that would not be enough for me to rely solely upon God if he shielded me from the pain of the experience. I would still have one false source of safety and security. I would still have one thing on which to lean and be able to say, "This will pull me through." I could still lean on myself.

Therefore God does not shield me from pain nor lessen its impact over time. He lets me hurt in order that I might find my sole source of safety, the only thing I can count on. The one rock in which I can hide is him. Isn't that how I'm supposed to live when I claim Jesus as my Savior? Thomas à Kempis put it this way:

> When a man of good will is afflicted, tempted, and tormented by evil thoughts, he realizes clearly that his greatest need is God, without Whom he can do no good. Saddened by his miseries and sufferings, he laments and prays. He wearies of living longer and wishes for death that he might be dissolved and be with Christ. Then he understands fully that perfect security and complete peace cannot be found on earth.[2]

Pain and suffering pry my hands off of everything in which I trust in order that I might trust in Christ alone. The Bible says four times, "The righteous person shall live by faith" (Habakkuk 2:4; Romans 1:17; Galatians 3:11; Hebrews 10:38). Habakkuk first penned these words during a time of national crisis. The country in which he lived, the ancient kingdom of Judah, was about to be overrun by a godless and bloodthirsty army. As their enemy troops gathered around the capital city, and stories of the atrocities spread, Habakkuk turned to the Lord and asked, "How long, O LORD, must I call for help? But you do not listen!" (1:2). After listening to Habakkuk describe the ruthless tactics of the invading Babylonians, the Lord replied, "Look at the proud! They trust in themselves, and their lives are crooked; but the righteous will live by their faith" (2:4). The righteous will live by their faith. Faith isn't a crutch to help in hard times or a salve to make me feel better when I'm blue. To live by faith means depending upon God and God alone for everything. I don't just trust him to get my soul to heaven; I must plunge myself on him as the only thing I need. When bad things fill my life, he allows me to find out how much progress I'm making toward making these words a reality.

In the process, God also refines and purifies my faith. As I mentioned a few pages ago, many of our prayers revolve around the hope that God will make our lives in this world more pleasant and secure. Yes, I'm supposed to pray about everything and pour out all my anxieties before his throne, but I must not fall into the trap of believing in God only *for* something. I've crossed the line when I believe in him in the hope he'll make my marriage stronger, my life feel more complete, or my kids stay out of trouble. Some even so pervert faith that they make God a road to wealth and prosperity. Jesus and the cross become little more than a means to an end, a way to get what we really want.

When God allows suffering to fill my life, when he refuses to take it away or lessen its pain, he is stripping away all my false ideas of what it means to trust in him. I'm not supposed to believe in him for what he will do for me. If I do, I'm still the center of my universe where God serves me; I don't serve him. Yet the call of the cross is to deny myself, take up my cross, and follow Jesus. Jesus does not call me to believe in order that he might make me happier or more secure. He calls me to believe because he is the way, the truth, and the life. He alone is God. He alone has the words of eternal life. Where else could I possibly go?

Does that mean I'm supposed to entrust my life to him even if it does me no good at all in this world? Of course. This is the definition of faith. This is the faith that not only enables me to survive the hardships inherent in living in a fallen world but it also gives me the power and grace to take the next step, to go forward and continue to live even when I thought doing so was impossible. A friend who recently lost her twenty-one-year-old daughter told me that her greatest struggle was accepting that the world did not stop when her daughter died. Life kept rushing forward. I don't know about the rushing part, but I know that this process of coming to grips with a good God who does not shield us from bad things is not complete until I, too, move forward with life. I think this may be the hardest step of all, a step only made harder by the fact that God rarely, if ever, explains why life took the turn it did. But because this entire journey is a journey of faith, what else would you expect?

PART FOUR

HOW CAN MY LIFE GO ON FROM HERE?

It doesn't matter, really, how great the pressure is, it only matters where the pressure lies. See that it never comes between you and the Lord — then, the greater the pressure, the more it presses you to his breast.

— HUDSON TAYLOR

CHAPTER 19

NO ANSWER BUT GOD

Throughout the book of Job, the title character had only one request. He wanted to stand before the Almighty and ask him why he'd become his enemy. "If only I knew where to find God," Job said, "I would go to his throne and talk with him there. I would lay out my case and present my arguments. Then I would listen to his reply and understand what he says to me" (Job 23:3-5). Job declared that if he could just talk with God, he would receive a fair hearing. "Fair and honest people can reason with [God]," he told his comforters, "so I would be acquitted by my Judge" (Job 23:7).

Job's words struck the three men beside him as blasphemous. In their eyes, God had already spoken. Actions always speak louder than words, and God's actions made it clear to them that Job had already been tried and convicted. "How can a mere mortal stand before God and claim to be righteous?" Bildad shouted back at him. "Who in all the earth is pure?" (Job 25:4). He's right. No one on earth is pure. No one is righteous. Romans 3:23 tells us that everyone on earth has sinned and comes short of the glory of God. Yet Job didn't seek an audience with God in order to claim to be the only person who had never sinned. Of course he was a sinner like everyone else on the planet, but he'd sought God's forgiveness. He loved the Lord. He knew the kind of relationship he'd enjoyed with God. He knew his own integrity and how diligently he'd sought the Lord. How could it all count for nothing? How could God turn his back on one who clung so desperately to him by faith?

Job couldn't find the answer. Again, he didn't know anything about the conversation in heaven between God and Satan. An angel didn't zip down to earth to tell Job his life was now a test case for why people will follow the Lord. All Job knew was how close God had once been and how silent heaven was now. God had turned away and built a wall between the two of them. If Job could just get God's attention, if the Lord would listen to him for even a short time, Job knew everything would be set right. And if God examined Job's life and found his integrity to be nothing but an act, Job was willing to accept any punishment God might dish out. "Have I lied to anyone or deceived anyone?" Job asked. "Let God judge me on the scales of justice, for he knows my integrity" (Job 31:6). All he wanted was an audience with God. "I would lay out my case and present my arguments. Then I would listen to his reply and understand what he says to me" (Job 23:3-5).

When we go through suffering, we can relate to Job's words. We just want to know what God is doing and why he has let our lives take this turn. The only one with the answer never speaks. A paper from heaven with a detailed plan for our lives never shows up in the mailbox. All we hear is silence, leaving us to grope in the dark for answers. We keep asking because we can't do much besides ask. *Am I being punished? Have I done something offensive in your sight, God? What possible purpose can these bad things serve?* If only he would answer. If he would just give us a hint as to what is going on. Any word would be better than nothing at all.

That's what Job thought until God gave him his request. The last five chapters of the book of Job record God's response to the conversation between Job and his three comforters. Apparently, God had been listening. Job said he wanted to confront God, so the Lord of the universe gave him the opportunity. "Do you want to argue with the Almighty?" God asked Job. "All right," he went on to say, "here's your opportunity." Job received the chance we all want. Job had God's full and undivided attention. Now Job could let his questions fly and present his case before God. At long last he could tell God how unfair things had been over the last several months or years or however long Job's suffering lasted.

There was just one little catch. Before God would answer Job's questions, he had a few of his own. "Where were you," God asked, "when I laid the foundations of the earth? Tell me, if you know so much. Do you know how its dimensions were determined and who did the surveying?" (Job 38:4-5). Job didn't respond. God fired off a few more. "Where were you when I laid the foundations of the universe? Do you know how it all fits together? Did you help survey it? And can you even tell me how it all works now? Tell me, Job, if you can," God asked.[1] Essentially, God had but one question. He asked it of Job, and it still echoes down to us in the silence from heaven in our times of suffering: *Who are you, a mere mortal, to question the actions of God?* "I'm God," he tells us. No explanations. No day in court where we get to present our case about how unfair he's been to us. No "I'm sorry you had to go through so much pain." Only this: I am God.

God kept asking Job questions. Four of the last five chapters of Job consist of nothing more than one question fired off after another. Not only does God stop Job in his tracks by showing his true character, he goes on to ask Job how he could question God's wisdom. "Do you know when the mountain goats give birth?" God asks. "Can you hitch a wild ox to a plow?" Before Job can utter a sound, God continues. "Have you given the horse its strength? . . . Are you the one who makes the hawk soar? . . . Is it at your command that the eagle rises to the heights to make its nest?" (Job 39:1,10,19,26,27). These questions about the animal kingdom strike us as a little odd until we listen to the real question running through them. In effect, God asked Job how much he even understood of the animals. Could he control them? Did he design their life cycle? Did he make them what they are? We never hear Job's answer, but we know what it is. No, no, and no. Listen as God whispers, "If you can't understand why I made the animals the way I did, how can you even begin to understand why I do what I do in your life?"

God doesn't have to come out and say it, but we can still hear him. He tells us that he knows what he is doing even if we don't. God's wisdom exceeds ours to the degree a redwood exceeds the size of an amoeba. About the time we think we can figure him out, we need to take a step outside. Where were we when the foundations of all the universe were laid? We think we have life and the world figured out, but meteorologists using the latest in computer technology can't even accurately predict the weather a few days in advance. Something as simple as the wind and the rain still go beyond our understanding. How much more so does God? And if we can't understand the workings of the physical universe, why would we assume we could understand the workings of the spiritual universe? Suffering hits and we want answers. God gives only one: I am God and I know what I am doing.

God displayed his power and majesty and reminded Job of his infinite wisdom, but he still wasn't finished. "Then the Lord said to Job, 'Do you still want to argue with the Almighty? You are God's critic, but do you have the answers?'" (Job 40:1-2). At this point Job crawled out from under the rock where he must have been hiding and muttered, "I am nothing—how could I ever find the answers? I will put my hand over my mouth in silence. I have said too much already"

(Job 40:3-5). Lots of people scream out against what they see as God's injustice. They accuse him of being unfair, unkind, unloving. When God steps onto the scene, every tongue will be silenced. Romans 3:19 says that God will shut every mouth when all the world stands before him in judgment. No one will be able to yell accusations or present his or her case before God. Every tongue will stick to the roof of its mouth. Job's did. The most righteous person on the face of the earth stood before God in stunned silence and shame. Who can argue with God?

Or who can control him? That was God's next question. He called Job's attention to two animals that people of Job's day feared above all others: behemoth and leviathan (possibly a hippopotamus and a crocodile). All right, God said to Job, jump down in the water with these two and let's see how you fare. Can you control either of them? Can you get them to do your bidding? These two animals had the same effect on Job's generation as the killer shark in *Jaws* had on mine. God invited Job to show how strong and mighty he was by reining either in. Can you do it, Job? God wanted to know. Of course not. God's message was clear: If you can't control a couple of animals, how could you ever assume you could control me?

We think we can control God. From time to time, I'll tune in to the local Christian television station to hear some evangelist straining over a pile of prayer requests, telling me how God must bless me if I'll just mail in a check. Most of us aren't that crass, yet deep down we assume we can get God to bless us if we live the right kind of life. We just know he will smile on us and shower us with good things if we are sincere enough in our faith. As one of my friends said in frustration over the constant downward spiral of his life, "I've lived for God, I've made sacrifices for his work, and this is the thanks I get." In response, God takes us out into animal world. If we are honest, we don't even need to see anything as big and frightening as an agitated hippo or a hungry croc. I can't get my dachshund to stop barking; what makes me think my actions can in any way force the Sovereign Lord over all creation to do anything?

That is ultimately God's question to Job and the rest of us as we complain about the way God runs the universe. He asks, If you can't even control some dumb animals, what makes you think you can control me? By the time God finished making his point, Job said,

> My ears had heard of you
> > but now my eyes have seen you.
> Therefore I despise myself
> > and repent in dust and ashes. (Job 42:5-6)

"I despise myself," he says. "I repent." What else could he say?

Here's what surprises me about this encounter. God didn't answer even one of Job's questions, but once Job saw God in his majesty, the questions no longer mattered. He no longer needed the opportunity to present his case before the Almighty. God didn't have to explain himself. Even though God never said one thing that Job longed to hear, simply coming face-to-face with the awesome power and majesty of God was enough. Job could now get up from his pile of ashes, put his regular clothes back on, and go forward with his life. He still hurt. His children were still dead. All his wealth still lay in ruins, but his life could now go on. God spoke. Job found himself in dead silence before God's power and might. And it was enough.

The final two paragraphs of the book of Job tell us that God restored Job's fortunes, even giving him twice as much as he had before. Some say this takes away the power of the book of Job. He didn't go forward, he got to go back. God restored his old life, even giving him another ten children. Job lived long enough to enjoy grandchildren and great-grandchildren. Sure, God tested Job, found

NO ANSWER BUT GOD

him to be faithful, then paid him off again in the end. Most of us will never be so lucky.

Yet the end of the book of Job never gives us a timetable. God may have restored Job's fortunes all at once, or it may have taken the next 140 years Job lived for his wealth to double his pre-disaster levels. I think the latter is closer to the truth. Even though Job and his wife enjoyed ten more children and later a house full of grandchildren, ten graves still lay behind the main house. The joy of his family would always be tempered by the grief for those who died and the thoughts of what might have been. Yes, his fortunes were restored, but life never really went back to normal, at least not the normalcy he had before. Job didn't go back; he went forward.

As we wrestle with coming to grips with the bad things God allows to flood over our lives, we must make the same decision. We must go forward. Suffering leaves a huge void in our lives. The pain intensifies and all we want is to go back to the way life used to be. If we could just change some of our choices and undo the damage. If we could just get our lives back. But we can't. Life never goes in reverse. We then face a choice. Either we can sit and wish for days gone by, or we can go forward. It isn't easy, but it is necessary.

The only way we can go forward is to once and for all come face-to-face with the God who holds the universe in the palm of his hand and discover, like Job, that just knowing he is God is enough. I know it doesn't sound very satisfying. We want more. We feel as if we can't go forward until we have some closure. Knowing that God is at work in our pain, and trusting in his wisdom to do what is best, still doesn't take the pain away. Nothing will. Nor do we have any assurance that tomorrow will be better than today. The trials and pains of today may be nothing in light of what could come next. When we see someone go through one horrific trial after another, we wonder how much one person can take. There is no answer, nor is there a maximum suffering

HOW CAN A GOOD GOD LET BAD THINGS HAPPEN?

quota we reach making us exempt from future trials. In this life we will have trouble, Jesus said. He didn't say how much and he never explained why. The world persecuted him and we can assume it will do the same to all who follow him. Why God doesn't change this Jesus left a mystery.

Yet there is one assurance we have: God is God. After all the tears and the questions and the angry screams toward heaven, God is still God. He created the universe and he holds it together now. Nothing else is certain. Nothing else is sure. Only God. Now in spite of the pain we've gone through in the past, in spite of the bad hands we've been dealt, it is time to go forward, trusting in the knowledge that he knows what he is doing, and resting in his care.

CHAPTER 20

I STILL WANT ANSWERS

That last chapter ended too easily. As I read back over it, I find that I still have a few questions of my own. Job's conversation with God might have ended, but that doesn't mean mine has. When I read those last five chapters of Job, I feel a little jealous. At least God gave Job an audience. He might not have answered Job's questions, but at least he showed up. How could that not be enough for Job to accept his present fate as God's plan and get on with life? But I'm not Job. God hasn't appeared to me. Just reading God and Job's conversation in the last five chapters of the book doesn't cut it for me. God is God, he can do whatever he wants, now deal with it? I'm sorry, I need something more. I need more than a line that sounds like my old football coach yelling at the guy on the ground with a messed-up ankle to get up and shake it off. It doesn't work in the world in which I live.

Is that really the point of the book of Job? God is God, deal with it? He can do whatever he wants, stop complaining? Where is God's mercy that the rest of the Bible talks about? Where is the compassion? Where is the love of God that goes beyond human understanding? This "deal with it" kind of love I can't understand. Here's the most godly person in the world, and he loses everything, including ten children. For who knows how long, he endures insults from the people around him. And all God says to comfort the one he points to as a shining example of virtue and righteousness is, "Where were you when I laid the foundations of the earth?" (Job 38:4).

I don't mean to be a spoiled child, but I need something more. The end of Job might be all hunky-dory for people who never lived through anything bad, but for the rest of us it falls flat. If we're going to go forward with life, not just go back to our daily routine but actually go forward with God, we need some sense that our suffering is somehow worth the pain. We also need an assurance that justice will be done. I don't want to use the word *repayment*, but in a sense that's what we need. We also need relief from the hurt. Even after the initial incident, the lingering effects of "bad things from the hand of God" stick with us for a lifetime. Some things we never really get over. But we want to. We want help. We need relief. Then there's the anger. When people hurt us, naturally we get mad. What do we do when God hurts us and we feel genuinely ticked off at him? I want to go forward. I want to be like Job and get on with life and my relationship with God. Maybe I will someday, but hearing nothing more from God than "Where were you when I laid the foundations of the earth?" doesn't lift me off the canvas.

Job got on with his life, but I have to wonder how he acted toward the Sabeans and Chaldeans who raided his ranch, stole his flocks, and killed his servants. Did he forgive them, or did he try to bring them to justice? I wonder if Job was like the guy I saw on the six o'clock news last night. He was the night's big story. The man sat in front of his house clutching an 8 x 10 photo of his sister. She died the night before when a drunk driver plowed into the front of her pickup truck. Apparently, the police had already been warned of the drunk's erratic driving. Another vehicle called 911 when the drunk driver almost sideswiped his car. Sheriff's deputies started their pursuit, but they arrived too late. The drunk driver swerved into oncoming traffic and hit another vehicle. He walked away from the wreck; one woman did not. Now her brother sat in front of his house on the evening news, clutching her picture. "I have just one request," he told the camera. "I want to walk into that jail and show that guy this picture and ask him, 'Was that drink worth it? Was your drink worth killing my sister over?'"

Most likely the guy on the news will never get his request. When the drunk driver goes on trial for vehicular homicide or perhaps second-degree murder, the victim's brother will be there. His sister's photo may not be in his hands, but he'll carry her into the courtroom simply by his presence. By this point, he'll have another request. He'll ask the judge to lock this killer away for a very long time. Once again, he'll want to make sure the drunk driver realizes what he took away from the family. He didn't just get behind the wheel of a car when his blood alcohol level doubled the legal limit; his poor choice cost this brother and the rest of the family the life of someone they loved. Nothing the judge can do and nothing the drunk driver can say will take that away. At best, the one responsible will experience at least some small measure of the pain he has inflicted on others. If he doesn't, not only the family but the entire community will say that justice has not been done.

Unless justice prevails, how can anyone go forward after his sister dies needlessly because someone was too cheap to call a cab or too stubborn to hand his keys to a designated driver? How much justice does there need to be for real closure to take place? As long as the man clutches his sister's picture, as long as he wants the drunk driver to feel the pain he feels and experience the loss he has to live with every day, no prison sentence will be long enough. Ten years, twenty years, thirty years, it won't matter. He'll be back at every parole hearing, retelling his story, asking once again, "Was that drink worth the price of my sister's life?" Hearing God boom out the questions he asked Job may not be enough to make us go forward, but neither will waiting for justice to repay us for the pain we've experienced.

The pain. Maybe that's what I find so unsatisfying about God's response to Job. We know that God restored Job's life. After he prayed for his three friends, real comforters showed up. All his sisters and brothers and former friends came to Job's home bringing gifts of money, gold rings, and food. People always bring food when they come to cheer us up. They came to "console him and comfort him because of all the trials the Lord had brought against him" (Job 42:11). The book makes it sound as if these people showing up made everything all right. They came with their casseroles and roasts and ham — er, they probably didn't bring ham since pigs aren't kosher — but they came with all their food and their get-well cards and their "I'm so sorrys," and Job perked right up.

If he did, the story can't be true.

Pain doesn't go away that easily. It doesn't for people who live in the real world; I can't imagine it did for Job. The pain of suffering, especially the pain of grief, not only grips our souls, it pulls us into ourselves. Walls go up and we feel ourselves being separated from those around us. We feel alone, yet we need the noise of other people around us. The conversations we hear, conversations about ball games and elections and the upcoming fall television season, don't interest us in the least. *How could anyone care about anything so trivial at a time like this?* we wonder. Yet, somehow, their presence helps us from falling even further into ourselves. That's the real danger of suffering. We may be pulled behind the walls it builds, where we will be completely isolated, completely lost in ourselves.

But that's not the worst of it. Within the pain of suffering and grief always lies the temptation to become self-absorbed. Not only do we feel pain, we begin to concentrate on how much the pain belongs to us. As our focus narrows to ourselves, we begin to think and say, "Oh, how sad I am" and "Oh, I'm in so much pain" and "Oh, life has been unfair to me." We stop thinking about the person who died and made us sad or the source of our pain. Everything becomes about us. Even though suffering makes us want to get away from everyone, the temptation to become self-absorbed makes us crave people's sympathy. In some sick way we almost feed off it. It's ugly. Temptation always is. I wouldn't even bring it up if I hadn't given in to it.

When I was in the seventh grade, Joe, one of the guys on our wrestling team, a guy I practiced against almost every day, hung himself. Whether it was an accident or suicide no one ever told us. The school allowed everyone who felt they needed to attend Joe's funeral to go. They even bussed us to the church and cemetery. Because Joe's services provided an opportunity to skip class, everyone in the seventh grade went. And how we carried on. All of us wept and cried and mourned as though our best friend in the world had died. It was hard for us to think about the mother and father who now had to deal with their twelve-year-old son's death for the rest of their lives. Most of us, or at least me, focused more on how sad we were because something sad had happened to us. We weren't crying as much for Joe as we were for ourselves.

This isn't just self-pity. It goes far deeper into a self-absorption that feels almost noble. Pain and grief don't have to degenerate into something so ugly. Maybe they don't for most people, only for those who are weak like me. But the temptation is always there, always lurking. Once we give in to it, there is no limit to the depths it will take us. At the beginning of the book, when we first started talking about accepting bad things from the hand of God, I never defined what those bad things might be because no definition would do. The more we allow pain to make us self-absorbed, the lower the threshold of bad becomes. The smallest inconvenience immediately reaches epic proportions. Then everything is bad. All of life is unfair. I'm always in pain, always suffering.

I think that may be why God's response to Job sounds so harsh to those who hurt. What appears to be harsh and cruel is necessary to pull us out of ourselves. God is merciful and near to the broken-hearted, but his compassion isn't pity. He doesn't pat us on the head and say, "There, there." Nor does he tell us to grow up, get up, and stop whining. By displaying his power and majesty, God not only leaves us silent, he resets our perspective. He refocuses our attention away from ourselves and toward his eternal purposes. It sounds harsh, but it is necessary. Remember, God also sent friends and family to Job's house to console him. Mercy accompanies truth.

I still have one little problem, one final obstacle I find I have to overcome. God can change my perspective, he can do all the things I've described in this chapter, yet deep down one hurt remains, and that hurt is God. I have trouble getting over the thought that he allowed this hurt to hit me in the first place. I don't know how else to phrase this than to say that as I reach the end of this journey, I have trouble forgiving God for what he has allowed to happen to me, for allowing sin to take its natural course. I know that last sentence sounds wrong, but I don't know any other way to describe getting over the anger toward God that pain and suffering can cause. Please don't take the word *forgive* to imply that God's done anything wrong. He hasn't. Nor does he owe us some sort of apology. As Creator he has the right to do with us and to us anything he desires. He may look cruel and harsh at times, but that's only because we don't understand what he is doing. A surgeon would look cruel and harsh cutting open someone's abdomen and removing organs if we didn't understand the concept of an appendectomy. Children get mad at doctors and nurses for sticking them with needles. The doctors and nurses don't owe the child an apology; the child needs to get over his desire to stick them back. In working toward our ultimate good, God often inflicts us with pain or, at the very least, refuses to shield us from the pain life dishes out. Before we can fully accept bad things from God and move forward in our relationship with him, we have to get over the desire to hurt him back. We have to get loose from our anger toward him.

I know, we're not supposed to get mad at God. A lot of verbs describe our relationship with him: *follow, trust, love, obey.* Harboring bitterness doesn't usually make the list. Besides, how do we tell the one who gave his Son for our souls that the thought of him fills us with sadness and hostility? Won't lightning fall from the sky? No, it's much easier to do what we usually do: bury the feelings, push them away, pretend they don't exist. After all, what kind of faith do I have if I react with anger rather than gentle trust in God? It's much easier to put on the front, play the part, go through the motions, and hope form will soon follow function.

Unfortunately, it doesn't work. Pretending our feelings don't exist only poisons our relationship with God. Cynicism replaces joy. We avoid God by distancing ourselves from the people who remind us of him. Because God has hurt us, we start taking jabs at him through acts of disobedience. Usually we start small, like dropping out of church or going back to old habits we had before Christ changed our lives. If we keep going down this path long enough, there's no limit to what we might do. Although we would never say it verbally, you can almost hear our actions scream, "Take that, God." Even as we strike back at God, we carry the fear that we've gone so far God won't take us back. Deep down we want him to take us back. Even as we try to shove him away, our souls want to cling to him.

So what do we do? How do we deal with and move past the anger we feel inside? We must start by doing what I said in chapter 7: get honest. As long as I keep my anger bottled up inside, I can pretend it doesn't exist and bury it deeper and deeper within my soul. Then

I can keep up the front, the facade, while the distance between God and me grows greater and greater. I need to come clean, bare my soul before God. No games, no fronts, just outright honesty. I'll never go forward until I do.

Which brings us back to where we were before. Job got honest with God, and all God said in return was, "Where were you when I laid the earth's foundations?" If you listen closely enough, you can hear another question: "Who are you that I owe you an explanation?" I know, this takes us right back to where we were at the beginning of the chapter, but rather than push God's words aside, think about them for a moment. What kind of explanation does God owe us beyond what he has already given? We become angry with God when life doesn't turn out the way we expect, when it feels as if God let us down. But has he?

Someone we love dies and we wonder why God didn't do anything to prevent it. What exactly did we think he would do? Look around. Everyone dies. Everyone—young, old, infants, children, middle-aged men, and little old ladies. Everyone dies and everyone will die because of the presence of sin in the world. Why do we become angry with God when the world works the way it has worked since the day sin entered it? Yes, every death is cruel when it strikes someone we love. We ask God why he didn't do something. Of course he doesn't answer, but then again, why should he?

Why should God explain to us why the American economy has fallen into recession or, worse, when a large percentage of the world's population lives in poverty? Do we really expect God to feel bad about not providing the money we need to make a payment for a second car or to pay for our child's dance lessons when people by the millions go to bed hungry each night? Life is hard and suffering surrounds us and nothing turns out exactly the way we'd hoped. With time the cumulative effects of unanswered prayers and unmet expectations wear us down. We grow angry at God and finally tell him so. But didn't he already tell us this is how life would be? Were we paying attention when he said, "Here on earth you will have many trials and sorrows" (John 16:33)? Or did we think he wasn't serious when he warned us, "Everyone who wants to live a godly life in Christ Jesus will suffer persecution" (2 Timothy 3:12)? When we come to the sad realization that we aren't exempt from the trouble that comes from living in a fallen world, we want to know why these things are happening to us. *I am God; trust me even without explanations*, is all we hear in return.

Even though God sounds harsh, a gentle touch comes through. He doesn't push us away. "Trust me" isn't just the final word in the argument; it is a reminder of how God will not leave us, no matter how much we think we want him to.

CHAPTER 21

THE ULTIMATE STEP
FORWARD

The ten Booms didn't set out to be heroes. An eighty-four-year-old man and two women approaching retirement age don't usually seek danger and adventure. They never sat down and plotted ways to resist the Nazi invasion of Amsterdam, but when Gestapo agents ransacked the home of a Jewish neighbor, Casper and his daughters Corrie and Betsie didn't have any other choice. They did what came naturally for three devoted followers of Jesus. In November 1941, they undertook their first covert operation and helped their neighbor escape to a safe place in the countryside. With time, more and more people came to them for help. Corrie soon became an expert in the art of people smuggling. As time wore on and the Nazis increased their efforts to round up all the Jews in Holland, fewer safe places could be found. By 1943, their house became a hiding place for persecuted people seeking refuge.

On February 28, 1944, Jan Vogel knocked on the door of the ten Boom home with a familiar story. "My wife, they've arrested my wife for hiding Jews. Oh, you must help me. If only I can raise six hundred guilders; there's a policeman who can be bribed for that amount. You must help me! She'll be sent to the camps. . . ." The ten Booms helped him just as they helped everyone who knocked on their door. But Jan Vogel wasn't like all the other desperate people. He was a spy for the German secret police. Shortly after Corrie and Betsie gave him the money, there was another knock on the door. Soldiers stormed in, knocking Casper to the ground, bloodying Betsie's face, pulling Corrie out of bed where she was sick with the flu. Systematically, the agents destroyed the house looking for evidence, looking for Jews. In the midst of the flurry of activity Betsie caught her father's eye and gently pointed to a plaque above the fireplace. On it were three simple words: Jesus is victor.

The ten Booms' nightmare stretched through the night and on to the end of the war. Casper died in police custody shortly after his arrest. Betsie and Corrie were taken to the concentration camps, first to Vught and later to Ravensbrück. The latter was a death camp. A surviving diary of Ravensbrück describes the place very few people walked away from:

> Our entire possessions consisted of a tin plate, a tin pot, and a wooden spoon — virtually nothing else, not even a hairpin, washcloth, sewing kit, or anything else. . . . In a very short time I was covered from head to toe with large, festering wounds caused by filth, dog bites, and vitamin deficiency.
>
> In the sleeping quarters we lay without sheets or blankets; there were scarcely any windowpanes, thus we were in a constant draft. The worst thing was the cold; for every morning, often long before daybreak, we stood without coats or any protective covering in the cold.

Every day sick, underfed creatures would
collapse, whereupon they would be beaten. If they
could not get up, they were sent to the office after
roll call in order to be "sent to the infirmary,"
which meant being gassed.[1]

Faced with unbearable suffering, Corrie and Betsie ten Boom
didn't lash out at their captors; instead, they prayed. They never ques-
tioned the goodness or mercy of God; instead, they started a Bible
study inside a flea-infested dorm, a room so filthy not even the guards
would enter it. Neither ever screamed at heaven demanding answers.
They were too busy giving others hope. Late one night, Corrie snuck
out of her dorm to hide in the dark next to a line of 250 women
marching out of the camp. She stood and whispered a brief word of
encouragement to each as the line passed by. With so many people
hurting, Corrie never had time to think about herself.

The ten Boom sisters didn't understand the "why" of suffering,
except their own. Yet both knew that God brought them to a death
camp to point the way to heaven for those who might die at any
moment.[2] Years later, Corrie described her experience in her book *The
Hiding Place*:

> As the rest of the world grew stranger, one thing
> became increasingly clear. And that was the reason
> the two of us were here. Why others should suffer
> we were not shown. As for us, from morning until
> lights-out, whenever we were not in ranks for roll
> call, our Bible was the center of an ever-widening
> circle of help and hope. . . . The blacker the night
> around us grew, the brighter and truer and more
> beautiful burned the Word of God.

I would look about as Betsie read, watching
the light leap from face to face. More than
conquerors. . . . It was not a wish. It was a fact.
We knew it, we experienced it minute by minute—poor, hated, hungry. We are more than
conquerors. Not "we shall be." We are! Life in
Ravensbrück took place on two separate levels,
mutually impossible. One, the observable, external
life, grew every day more horrible. The other, the
life we lived with God, grew daily better, truth
upon truth, glory upon glory.[3]

Corrie ten Boom survived to tell her story. Her sister did not.
Betsie's health continued to deteriorate until she was taken to the
camp infirmary. No one told Corrie when she died. She had to dig
through a pile of corpses in a shower to find Betsie's broken body.
Four days after Betsie's death, Corrie was released. She never knew
why she was spared while her sister and father were not. In spite of the
horrors she faced, Corrie never harbored bitterness or anger against
her captors. It wasn't easy. One day God brought her face-to-face
with a cruel camp guard. As she looked into his eyes, she knew she
had to forgive him just as God in Christ had forgiven her. Corrie
ten Boom escaped the corrosive power of bitterness through a decision she and her sister had made when they were thrown into the
camps. Rather than see their experience as a horrible aberration, they
chose to accept it as an opportunity to be used by God to help those
in need. Corrie survived her nightmare by choosing to serve others
through her suffering.

My friend Lynn didn't set out to make an impression on anyone. While sitting at her father's bedside for hours without end, watching as the man who shaped her life battled cancer, Lynn had time to think and to pray. She prayed a lot. She prayed that God might grant her father some kind of miracle, she prayed for her mother as she faced the very real prospect of being alone for the first time in over fifty years, and she prayed for herself, for the strength to carry on. People came by the hospital to encourage Lynn and cheer up her family, but everyone knew how the story would end. The cancer came so quickly, and it was so advanced by the time doctors discovered it, nothing would be able to stop it.

Just one month earlier, Lynn's dad was driving a lawn mower across his acreage, taking care of his horses, and making plans for projects he hoped to complete around the house by the end of the summer. Before his cancer, Lynn went to visit him at least once a week and talked to him on the phone every few days. Their phone calls weren't the touching long-distance-telephone-commercial variety. She called him when she needed him to do something around the house she couldn't get her husband to tackle. Neither ever dreamed they would spend their summer in and out of hospitals. When Lynn started her summer break from teaching junior high students, she never thought she would bury her father before classes started again in the fall.

As the summer wore on and the inevitable drew closer, Lynn kept praying. The more she prayed, the more God expanded her horizons. She didn't pray only for her family's pain. One name kept coming to her mind: Michelle. Michelle was a member of Lynn's church. At one time she overflowed with excitement for God. Her light didn't burn so brightly these days. A conflict within the church burned Michelle and doused her excitement. She didn't go to church very often anymore. When she did, she acted as though she couldn't wait to leave.

The more time Lynn spent in prayer next to her father's bed, the more she prayed for Michelle. So one evening after spending the day at the hospital, Lynn called Michelle to let her know she'd missed her at church. More than that, she wanted to let her know she missed the fire, the excitement, the devotion Michelle once showed toward the Lord. Lynn wasn't trying to make any kind of impression. The more she prayed for Michelle, the more she knew she needed to call her to try to pull her back to Christ.

Michelle was floored. "I couldn't believe she even thought about me," was all she could say in response. "With all she's going through, why would she care about me?" The idea that someone going through so much pain would be so concerned about her touched her deeply. Lynn wasn't trying to touch Michelle. She just did what she knew she needed to do. She chose to serve others while she was suffering.

Phyllis didn't think she had anything to say that anyone would want to hear. She never felt she had any special insight into how to survive losing a husband. All she had was the experience. Her husband had died two years earlier after a long illness. He wanted to be buried near the rest of his family, and of course she granted his request. But the cemetery was more than a hundred miles from her house and she made the trip every couple of weeks. Eventually, she uprooted and bought a house in the same town as the cemetery. It wasn't just her husband's grave that brought her to town. Her only sister lived nearby, the closest family Phyllis had since Phyllis and her husband never had children. Even though two years had passed since her husband died, she couldn't talk about him without tears welling up in her eyes. Her poodle kept her company and protected her by barking wildly at every potential threat, real or imagined. Nothing filled the hole created by losing the man with whom she'd shared more than forty years. She got on with her life as best she could in a new town with new friends and a new church.

It didn't take long for Phyllis to get involved. Never one to sit on the sidelines, she made the church kitchen her own personal domain. When the church hosted its annual dinner for traveling carnival workers during the town's Jubilee Days, Phyllis was always in the middle of the activity. She would cook extra dishes to make sure every carny could eat his fill and take an extra plate of food back to his trailer. Every once in a while, the Sunday school director or the children's ministry director would try to talk Phyllis into teaching a children's class. She never did. Because she never had children of her own, she wasn't comfortable around them. She was quite content to attend church faithfully and help in the kitchen. It was her niche, her place to serve.

That is until the day her pastor called with a special request. He asked Phyllis to go with him to see a stranger, a woman named Evelyn, who had a familiar story. After protesting, Phyllis finally consented. All through the drive to Evelyn's house, Phyllis kept saying, "I don't have anything special to say; I don't know why you need me to come along." She wasn't complaining; she was just telling the truth as far as she could see it. But her pastor knew that Evelyn needed to connect with Phyllis. Two weeks earlier, Evelyn had buried her husband after he died suddenly of a heart attack. She found herself a widow at forty-six. Like Phyllis, Evelyn and her husband never had children. Now she was very alone.

A few minutes after Phyllis and her pastor walked through Evelyn's door, her apprehension disappeared. The woman with nothing special to say didn't need to say anything. As she listened to Evelyn's story, she saw herself and remembered everything she'd gone through over the previous two years. Phyllis didn't say much during that first visit.

She didn't have to. Just her presence said enough. Over the next several months, Phyllis and Evelyn spent more and more time together. Evelyn leaned heavily on her new friend to help her make hard decisions, like selling her dream home and moving into a smaller house she could take care of. Phyllis still never thought she had anything special anyone needed to hear. She chose to serve others suffering through the same nightmare she'd experienced. In the process, she worked through her own pain by helping someone else.

It doesn't have to be heroic. The stakes do not have to be life and death. Yet choosing to serve others in our suffering helps us see God's use of our pain for his good. He comforts us in all our afflictions in order that we might comfort others. We don't just suffer on behalf of others. This isn't martyrdom we're talking about. Rather, it is a simple choice to see even the bad things in our lives as opportunities for the finger of God to touch someone else. In the previous chapter, we explored the temptation inherent in all suffering: the temptation to withdraw within ourselves. Choosing to serve others as we suffer pulls us out of ourselves and focuses our attention on God's greater purposes. The choice doesn't necessarily make the pain any less painful, nor does it cause a light to come on so we suddenly understand why suffering must take place. But it can free us to go forward and to allow God to use for his good what the world meant as evil.

George MacDonald once said, "The Son of God suffered unto the death, not that men might not suffer, but that their sufferings might be like His."[4] When we choose to serve others in and through our suffering, we truly imitate the One who gave his life that we might live. Our sufferings do not end, but they become fully like his.

CHAPTER 22

THE FINAL CHAPTER
(IN MORE WAYS
THAN ONE)

L ife hurts. Life is hard. Life is full of trouble. Life is all of that and
more. But there's one thing life is not: This life, this physical existence, is not the final chapter in the lives of those who cling to Christ
by faith. "What we suffer now is nothing compared to the glory he
will give us later," Paul reminds us in Romans 8:18.

Paul penned those words not just to prepare us for the hard times
this life will hold but also to refocus our eyes on what lies beyond.
This world may be full of trouble, but our suffering won't last forever.
Once it ends, the good stuff begins. Reserved in heaven for everyone
who will entrust his or her life to Jesus Christ is an incredible treasure
that will never rust or corrode or fade away. As Romans 8:17 tells us,
"Since we are his children, we will share his treasures—for everything God gives to his Son, Christ, is ours, too." Ponder that thought
for a moment. All the treasures God gives his Son, he will give to us
as well. And they're waiting for us. The moment we go through the
last act of suffering this life can throw at us, we enter into the glories

of heaven.

And oh, how glorious it will be. Words can't even begin to capture its wonder. There will be no more death or sorrow or crying or pain. Not only will every trace of the evils of this world be gone, even their memories will pass. The Bible does speak of tears in heaven, tears God himself will reach down and wipe away with his gentle touch. The heavenly city itself radiates the glory of God. The streets are paved with pure gold as clear as glass with precious stones of every kind inlaid in the foundation. The river of life flows through the middle, where all who are thirsty can drink to their hearts' content. In this place there will be no night, no fear, only the glorious presence of God's love.

Thinking about heaven and all its glory makes me wonder, *Who wants it most? Who aches for it, dreams about it, longs to walk through its gates? Who would be first in line if the bus left tomorrow?* The answer is simple, but not as simple as it might at first appear. Since we've just spent twenty-one chapters talking about suffering, the answer has to be those who suffer. People this world beats up must long for the world to come. It makes sense. One of God's purposes in suffering is to wean us off this world. Therefore, the more we suffer, the less we want of this world and, by default, the more we want heaven.

I think my logic is impeccable. It is also wrong. This morning I read about a man in Tokyo who lives in a shack he built out of scraps from building sites. His lean-to is about the size of a refrigerator carton, although it does a better job of keeping the rain out. Inside he has an alarm clock, a tape player, and a sort-of bed. He calls the lean-to his home, although everyone else refers to him as homeless. The man hasn't always lived in a box next to Tokyo Bay. Before he lost his job, he lived in a high-rise apartment. Not anymore. Maybe not ever again. Now he lives in a box. I think his living arrangements fit Job's description of a bad thing from the hand of God. But living in a shack with an alarm clock and a tape player and a sort-of bed doesn't necessarily make a man long for heaven. All he really wants is a real house.

Suffering intense pain in this life doesn't always translate into a longing for a front-row seat before the throne of God. It may just leave us wanting at least five pain-free minutes. Constantly struggling with physical and emotional problems leaves us looking for some relief. If heaven offers it, great, we'll take it, but we're usually not in a big hurry to go ahead and die to take advantage of the offer. We talk a lot about heaven when a person dies—at least I talk a lot about heaven when I conduct someone's funeral. Most people expect at least a passing reference at some point during the service. Missing someone so badly our chest feels as though it will implode makes us want to see him or her again. But it doesn't always mean we desire the real experience of heaven.

Who, then, craves the treasures of heaven most?

A few years ago, I fulfilled a lifelong dream by taking the family to a small town in upstate New York, a town called Cooperstown. In the center of town, amid the rolling hills and tall trees, stood a redbrick building with these words over the main doors: National Baseball Hall of Fame. I had goose bumps while standing on the sidewalk waiting for the doors to open. My family didn't quite have the same eager expectation. In fact, no one else in the family—neither my wife nor our three daughters—cares much about baseball. I shot through the doors, dragging the four women in my life behind me.

Our first stop was the actual Hall of Fame, where the greatest legends of the game are memorialized with bronze plaques. I started to look calmly at each plaque in order, but the kid-in-a-candy-store finally got to me and I started rushing around looking for every player from my favorite baseball team. Because my favorite team started winning World Series championships in the twenties and still hasn't stopped, there were a lot of players' shrines to see. I was afraid I wouldn't have enough film to get pictures of them all. My wife stayed with me for about as long as it took to read Babe Ruth's and Lou Gehrig's statistics. She found a bench and sat back watching people. My three daughters eventually joined her. The oldest sat down after reading about Lefty Gomez, the youngest after Joe DiMaggio. By the time I found Mickey Mantle, I was all by myself. I didn't notice until I was ready to move on to the next exhibit.

The bronze plaques were only the beginning. Other rooms in the Hall made my spine tingle. Babe Ruth's bat was there, along with Yogi Berra's glove and the ball from Don Larsen's perfect game in the 1956 World Series. One exhibit had a baseball from every no-hitter thrown since the Hall opened. Nolan Ryan had his own special spot on the wall, with both a ball and the team cap from each of his seven no-hitters. I could go on forever, and if you love baseball as much as my daughters do, I've already gone on too long. A few hours into my family's Hall of Fame experience, we made our way into the Stadium Room. I jumped into one of the original stadium seats from Ebbets Field. Just out of my sight, all three of my girls grabbed the bars of a gate from old Comiskey Park and began banging their heads against it. They said their minds felt like Jell-O and they couldn't wait to get out of Cooperstown. I can't wait to go back.

I loved the National Baseball Hall of Fame because everything about it revolves around my favorite sport. My wife and daughters hated it, even though they don't hate baseball. They don't mind the game. Every year we go to a couple of games and everyone always has a good time. My girls especially enjoy the ice cream sundaes served in little batting helmets. But my wife and daughters don't love baseball. If anything, they're indifferent to it. They'll tolerate an inning or two on television, but finding themselves trapped in a maze of rooms where every exhibit revolves around baseball turned into a nightmare for them after a half hour or so. Now they know how I feel when my wife drags me to a craft store.

So who craves the treasures of heaven most? Most people think they want to go there someday. We read about streets of gold and gates of pearl, and it sounds like a place we would enjoy seeing. After all, it beats the alternative. But most of our ideas about heaven come more from speculation than from the Bible. The streets may be paved with gold, but no one stops to pry up a brick or two. Jesus said salt that loses its saltiness isn't good for anything but being thrown into the streets to be trampled upon by people. Gold in the streets of heaven tells us that all the things people crave the most in this world are absolutely worthless in the world to come. The King James Version of the Bible says something about there being mansions up there, and we can't wait to claim ours. But the word used in John 14:2 actually means *rooms*. Jesus said, "There are many rooms in my Father's home, and I am going to prepare a place for you" (NLT).

The gold doesn't matter, the mansion is actually a room in the Father's house, and the Bible never mentions big reunions with those who went before us. There's no biblical evidence that lost loves are reunited there for all eternity. In fact, when we think of eternity, we have to think outside the scope of our this-world experience. Heaven isn't a supersized, permanent version of our existence here. It is totally different, completely new. When God ushers in the eternal age, he also will create a new heaven and a new earth. This boggles my mind. He created the heavens and the earth, with all their splendor, in six days. Jesus has been working on the New Creation for the past two thousand years. If he can make the awesome wonder of a sunset over the Pacific Ocean off Pismo Beach in six days, imagine what awaits us!

God tells us what awaits us. Through the Bible he lets us know exactly what the treasure of heaven is. Once we see it, we'll know who craves it most. Listen to the words of Paul: "To me, living is for Christ, and dying is even better. . . . I'm torn between two desires: Sometimes I want to live, and sometimes I long to go and be with Christ" (Philippians 1:21,23). The treasure of heaven is Christ. He is our inheritance. He is the wonder of heaven.

So who longs for the treasures of heaven? Only those who love Jesus. They are the ones on whom the world loses its grip, especially as God weans us off of it through suffering. When trials hit, the things of this world become nothing but garbage, with no appeal to us at all, because our desire grows ever stronger for God himself. We don't merely want to know him; we want to lose ourselves in him, to be lost in his love and the wonder of his grace. But one day our suffering in this life will end completely. We will close our eyes in this world and open them in the very presence of God. As we bask in the glory of God's presence, we will know once and for all that "what we suffer now is nothing compared to the glory he will give us later" (Romans 8:18).

Yes, our bodies will be changed then. We won't feel any more pain. Backs won't creak and knees won't ache when the weather turns damp. All the restrictions of life in a mortal body will end. God will clothe us in his glory. Our bodies will become like Jesus' resurrected body. God does this to allow us to finally walk by sight and no longer by faith. We will see him face-to-face. We'll feel the warmth of his embrace and his tender touch as he wipes every tear from our eyes. Heaven may hold lots of wonders we may want to explore some day, but I doubt if anyone or anything will be able to pry us away from the arms of Christ. After loving him so long without ever seeing his face, after aching to finally be free of this flesh and be with him, we will never be able to get enough of him. He is the treasure of heaven. He is our inheritance. And he is the hope that allows us to go forward even when we would rather pull the covers over our heads and never get up. The hope of heaven isn't some religious notion to make us feel better at funerals; it is the ultimate reality, the final chapter, that makes all the other chapters make sense. People ask how they will ever get on with life after disaster strikes. This is the only answer I've found. This hope. This promise from God. This guarantee, which is heaven. Nothing else can satisfy. If this life is all there is, we have no hope. But because God has a final chapter awaiting us in his presence, we can live as though what we suffer now is nothing because of what lies ahead.

NOTES

CHAPTER 3: THE DANGER OF LIVING WITH A GOD I CAN'T FIGURE OUT

1. All the quotes of Job in this paragraph are paraphrases taken from Job 3 and other speeches of Job.
2. Paraphrase of Job 4:7-9.

CHAPTER 5: WHAT I ALWAYS FEARED

1. Visit www.persecution.com for fresh reports of those who suffer for Christ around the world.
2. C. S. Lewis, *A Grief Observed* (San Francisco: HarperSanFrancisco, 2001), 6–7.

CHAPTER 8: MUST GOD SEEM GOOD FOR ME TO BELIEVE?

1. C. S. Lewis, *God in the Dock* (Grand Rapids, MI: Eerdmans, 1970), 108.
2. George MacDonald, *At the Back of the North Wind* (Wheaton, IL: Christian Classics Ethereal Library, 1996), CCEL e-book edition, 16.

CHAPTER 10: WHY DOESN'T GOD DO SOMETHING (IF HE CAN)?

1. Agnolo di Tura, quoted in Russell Chandler, *Doomsday: the End of the World, A View Through Time* (Ann Arbor, MI: Servant, 1993), 117.
2. Harold S. Kushner, *When Bad Things Happen to Good People* (New York: Schocken, 1981), 58, emphasis added.
3. Martin Luther, *Table Talk,* trans. William Hazlett, section DCCCXIV, CCEL e-book edition.

CHAPTER 12: CRUEL

1. C. S. Lewis, *The Problem of Pain* (New York: Macmillan, 1962), 105.
2. Lewis, 105.

CHAPTER 13: WHERE MY FUTURE LIES

1. Paraphrase of John 11:21.

CHAPTER 16: DOES THE ROCK ENJOY BEING CHISELED INTO A STATUE?

1. William Hendricks, *Exit Interviews* (Chicago: Moody, 1993), 252.
2. *The Baptist Standard*, June 10, 2002.
3. Jon Walker, "Barna: Terrorist attacks did not change most Americans spiritually," http://www.pastors.com/articles/BlackTuesday.asp.
4. C. S. Lewis, *The Problem of Pain* (New York: Macmillan, 1962), 85.

CHAPTER 18: TOE-TO-TOE WITH OUR GREATEST ENEMY

1. C. S. Lewis, *The Pilgrim's Regress*, deluxe illustrated edition (Grand Rapids, MI: Eerdmans, 1981), 176.

2. Thomas à Kempis, *The Imitation of Christ* (Wheaton, IL: Christian Classics Ethereal Library, 1998), 23, http://ccel .org/k/kempis/imitation2/About.htm.

CHAPTER 19: NO ANSWER BUT GOD

1. Paraphrase of God's statements in Job 38.

CHAPTER 21: THE ULTIMATE STEP FORWARD

1. Carole C. Carlson, *Corrie ten Boom: Her Life, Her Faith* (Old Tappan, NJ: Revell, 1983), 107–108.

2. Carlson, 110.

3. Corrie ten Boom with John and Elizabeth Sherrill, *The Hiding Place* (New York: Bantam Books reissue edition, 1984), 179.

4. George MacDonald, quoted in C. S. Lewis, *The Problem of Pain* (New York: Macmillan, 1962), 7.

AUTHOR

MARK TABB has authored and coauthored more than twenty books. His March 2008 release, *Mistaken Identity*, debuted at number one on the *New York Times* best seller list. He also worked with Alec Baldwin on *A Promise to Ourselves* and with Stephen Baldwin on the 2006 *New York Times* best seller *The Unusual Suspect*. Mark's solo titles include the 2006 release *Living with Less, The Upside of Downsizing Your Life*, and the 2004 ECPA Gold Medallion finalist *Out of the Whirlwind*, along with many other titles.

Writing is only one small part of Mark's life. He and his wife have been married for more than twenty-five years, and have three daughters. When he is not writing, Mark pulls double duty with his local fire department, serving as both the chaplain and a volunteer firefighter. A 1986 graduate of the Criswell College in Dallas, Texas, Mark served as a pastor for sixteen years before quitting his day job to write full time in 2002. He and his family live in Indiana. Learn more at his website, www.marktabb.com, or contact him at mark@marktabb.com.

Deepen your walk with God with these other great NavPress titles!

Trusting God
Jerry Bridges
ISBN-13: 978-1-60006-305-3
ISBN-10: 1-60006-305-5

When unexpected situations arise that appear unjust, irrational, or even dreadful, we feel confused and frustrated. And before long, we begin to doubt God's concern for us or His control over our lives. If God were really in control, why would He allow bad things to happen to us? As you begin to explore the scope of God's power, you'll begin to acknowledge His loving control and trust Him more completely—even when life hurts.

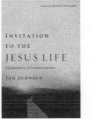

Invitation to the Jesus Life
Jan Johnson
ISBN-13: 978-1-60006-146-2
ISBN-10: 1-60006-146-X

It's easy to learn a little something about Jesus, but to encounter Him on a daily basis changes everything. No longer can we live with the same earthly behavior or attitude. Our focus becomes eternal. Jan Johnson helps you experience Jesus in such a way that His love-drenched, others-focused nature shapes your character.

Coffeehouse Theology
Ed Cyzewski
ISBN-13: 978-1-60006-277-3
ISBN-10: 1-60006-277-6

A relationship with God is central to life-breathing theology, but today's culture experiences a barrier of ignorance and misunderstanding of the church's mission. Through stories and illustrations, Ed Cyzewski builds a method for theology that is rooted in a relationship with God and His mission.

To order copies, visit your local Christian bookstore, call NavPress at
1-800-366-7788, or log on to www.navpress.com.
To locate a Christian bookstore near you, call 1-800-991-7747.

NAVPRESS○.